E IN RETURN BOX to remove this checkout from your record.
OID FINES return on or before date due.

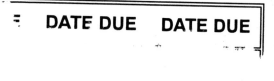

DATE DUE	DATE DUE	DATE DUE

Documenting Diversity:

A Report on the Conference on Documenting the Immigrant Experience in the United States of America

November 15-17, 1990

Immigration History Research Center
Saint Paul, Minnesota

UNIVERSITY OF MINNESOTA

Documenting Diversity:

A Report on the Conference
on Documenting the Immigrant Experience
in the United States of America

November 15-17, 1990

Prepared by
CDIE Planning Committee

Immigration History Research Center
Saint Paul, Minnesota

UNIVERSITY OF MINNESOTA

1991

ISBN 0-932833-12-8

Text preparation and design by Judith Rosenblatt

History Committee, Statue of Liberty/ Ellis Island Centennial Commission

JV
6405
1990
C. 2

CDIE Planning Committee

ACKNOWLEDGMENTS

Initial planning for the Conference on Documenting the Immigrant Experience was made possible by a grant from the Alfred P. Sloan Foundation to the History Committee of the Statue of Liberty/Ellis Island Centennial Commission. Subsequently, grants from the Statue of Liberty/Ellis Island Foundation, Inc., and the National Historical Publications and Records Commission funded the conference preparation, the conference itself, and postconference planning. A further grant from the NHPRC enabled preparation and distribution of this report. We gratefully acknowledge the vision of these agencies, which is helping us to realize our ideas.

The Immigration History Research Center, University of Minnesota, was responsible for administration of the 1990 conference and preparation of the final report.

CONTENTS

FINDINGS AND RECOMMENDATIONS

Immigration and ethnicity are major forces in American life. Until recently, however, they have been under-recognized and inadequately documented.[1] In November 1990 a group of historians and archivists convened the Conference on Documenting the Immigrant Experience to consider the state of ethnic archives and ethnic history. The meeting was inspired by a recognition of the imperative need for a collaborative effort to preserve and interpret the historical record of this basic dimension of the American experience.

At the conclusion of the conference the participants agreed on the following findings and recommendations:

1. Documentation of the immigrant experience is inadequate, fragmentary, and scattered; records are often intellectually inaccessible for research and physically at risk.

2. A national strategy to locate, preserve and make accessible the records of the immigrant experience in the United States is urgently needed. The strategy should encompass the following elements:

    a. The bulk of ethnic historical records currently remain outside of archival custody, where they face deterioration and eventual loss;

    b. The consciousness of historians, archivists, other professionals and the public at large needs to be raised about the risks facing ethnic and immigrant records and the need to preserve them;

    c. Improved communication among those who are responsible for the custody, use, and interpretation of the record of immigration and the ethnic experience is essential;

---

[1] The conference discussed at length the relationship between immigration and ethnicity. The sense of this discussion is reported in the notes from the Content Definition Workshop (page 12) and in the report on the final plenary session (page 16).

d.   Ethnic historical records must be brought into archival custody with improved intellectual and physical access to them;

e.   Efforts to preserve America's documentary heritage should be extended to the record of the immigrant and ethnic past by expanding financial resources and supporting actions that upgrade and enhance the curatorial care and physical environment of the records;

3. The experiences of the immigrants, as they themselves recorded them in words and images, should be presented through a variety of media (including a series of documentary volumes) for educational, research, and other purposes.

This report represents the initial formulation of a national strategy for documenting the immigrant and ethnic experience in America. It envisions the formation of a broad-based coalition of institutions to carry out these recommendations in collaboration. The Agenda for Action at the conclusion of this report elaborates on the means for implementing this program.

STEPS LEADING TO THE CONFERENCE

Immigration and ethnicity are no longer neglected dimensions of American history. Today, a new generation of scholars is busily engaged in telling the story of America's peopling as a vital component of the American experience. The re-opening of Ellis Island, America's premiere immigration depot in the late nineteenth and early twentieth century, as a monument to the newcomers who built America and as a museum to tell their story, is testimony to the public interest in this important chapter in our republic's history. And the United States is once again the goal of a new immigration, except now airports have replaced Ellis Island as portals of entry. The presence of many newcomers makes even more vivid and compelling the need to document the immigrant experience over the span of almost five centuries.

Historians who wish to recount the experiences of immigrants in their books and articles often encounter serious obstacles. The sources for doing immigration history, even when they have been collected, tend to be dispersed and sometimes intellectually inaccessible. The valiant efforts of archivists, librarians, and the guardians of countless ethnic and local historical collections have saved from destruction a vast array of documents on different immigrant groups. Too often this documentation remains at risk because the resources for employing professional staff and properly housing such collections are simply inadequate.

Even those immigrant records that are well housed and cared for are accessible only to the relatively few scholars who have the time, skills (including language), and funding for extended research in various repositories. The compilation and publication of a documentary history of immigration that would make such records readily available to a broad public is therefore badly needed and long overdue. Conceived of as an internal history of immigration, such a documentary history would allow the immigrants to tell their stories across the centuries in their own words, translated from the languages in which those words were written, spoken, or sung.

These perceptions of needs and advocacy of remedies are neither entirely original nor entirely without precedent. One may, for example, find them foreshadowed in the documentary work done on ethnic history under the Federal Writers' Project of the 1930s as well as Louis Adamic's contemporaneous project, "From Plymouth Rock to Ellis Island." Impetus for the Project on Documenting the Immigrant Experience (PDIE), however, developed from the discussions of the History Committee,[2] established in 1983 to advise the Statue of Liberty/ Ellis Island Centennial Commission and Statue of Liberty/Ellis Island Foundation, Inc., on matters of preservation and interpretation. As well as restoring the monuments, the committee aspired to exploit the occasion of the centennial for the purpose of advancing scholarship and popular education regarding immigration and ethnic history.

With a seed grant from the Alfred P. Sloan Foundation, the History Committee initiated several scholarly projects, among them a documentary history of American immigration. Recognizing the complexity of the project, committee members identified as an immediate and necessary goal securing support to hold a conference of appropriate scholars to design and approve the project concept. Two committee members, Victor Greene and Alan Kraut, were deputized to develop the idea and a proposal to seek funding for the conference.

The Statue of Liberty/Ellis Island Foundation then made a grant to the History Committee for a planning conference. Meanwhile—and independently—the idea of a documentary history of immigration had surfaced in the deliberations of the National Historical Publications and Records Commission. Upon learning of their mutual interest, the History Committee and the NHPRC engaged in discussions, which resulted in a more comprehensive agenda. Members of the History Committee met with Nancy Sahli, Mary Giunta, and Roger Bruns of the NHPRC in Washington, D.C., in August 1988. From these conversations emerged a plan for a documentary history project within the context of a larger undertaking of documenting the immigrant experience. Clearly, archivists and librarians as well as historians had to be involved in a systematic effort to locate, collect, preserve, and make physically and intellectually accessible sources on a myriad of immigrant groups. Only when the universe of records for any particular group had been established could an editor proceed confidently with the compilation of a documentary history.

---

[2] See Appendix A, the conference program, for a list of the committee members.

THE CONFERENCE

By 1988, the History Committee had received support for the planning conference from two sources: a grant from the Statue of Liberty/Ellis Island Foundation, Inc., and a matching grant from the NHPRC. By the terms of the latter award "The Immigrant Experience in America Conference" would "concern itself with a national strategy for archival preservation and documentary publications in the area of the immigrant experience" (NHPRC grant letter, December 2, 1988). Furthermore, the NHPRC mandated a planning committee to be composed of professional archivists, immigration historians, and at least one documentary editor. The primary product of the conference was to be a published conference report, widely distributed with "recommendations for a national strategy for archival preservation and documentary publication of the records of immigration to the United States" (ibid.).

The conference planning committee, selected by the History Committee, approved by the NHPRC, and chaired by Rudolph Vecoli, was headquartered at the Immigration History Research Center, University of Minnesota. In addition to two meetings to plan the conference, the committee conducted its business by telephone and mail. Its members selected the conference site and time, devised its intellectual structure, and identified and invited the participants.

The planning committee, in consultation with NHPRC staff, decided that the Conference on Documenting the Immigrant Experience (CDIE) should bring together no more than forty-five invited participants (forty-two attended), representing the specialties of immigration history, archival management, and documentary editing, and including as comprehensive a spectrum of immigrant/ethnic groups as possible. In order to maximize the input of participants, a conference format of formal papers, workshops, and plenary sessions was designed to elicit their ideas and expertise. The objective was to define the needs and problems in documenting the immigrant experience and to identify possible solutions. The conference report was to include an action agenda addressing specific tasks that would provide the basis for funding proposals to foundations, public agencies, and publishers. Anticipating this outcome, a select number of representatives of funding agencies and publishers were invited to send participant-observers to the conference (eight attended).

5

On November 15-17, 1990, fifty individuals from across the United States and other countries, including Canada, Sweden, Italy, and Germany, gathered at the IDS Oak Ridge Conference Center in Chaska, Minnesota, for the Conference on Documenting the Immigrant Experience. The participants[3] were selected to represent a broad diversity of research fields, archival and historical institutions, and ethnic backgrounds. Among the participants were curators of small and large immigration collections, as well as non-immigration repositories with a high volume of immigrant records; teachers and writers of immigration history; editors of journals with an interest in immigration history; documentary editors with experience in foreign language records; as well as persons knowledgeable about immigrant-related documentation in foreign repositories.

While it was impossible because of the limitation of size to invite representatives of each ethnic group, larger immigrant groups, both new and old, from most continents were represented. The secluded conference setting provided ample opportunity for participants and observers to interact and discuss the issues informally at meals, evening gatherings, and walks around the IDS Conference Center pond.

The conference content was divided equally between issues the committee considered vital to archivists and those of most concern to historians, which also provided a continuum from collecting through publishing the records of the American immigration experience. Following a keynote address to provide the background that led to the conference and to state the issues to be addressed, five conference participants presented papers.[4] Each addressed one of the main conference topics and provided the framework for the discussion of issues by participants in workshops.

Following the papers, the conference broke up into workshops. All participants were asked to attend at least two workshops, one from each of two concurrent series. While conference participants were invited to express preferences for workshops, the planning committee assigned each participant to a workshop, taking into account the need for balance among disciplines and experience at each workshop. Topics were the same as those presented in the papers, and participants were encouraged to agree, disagree, refine, and build on the issues each speaker raised. The archival workshops were held on Friday afternoon, November 16, while those associated with the documentary publication took place on Saturday morning, November 17.

---

[3] See Appendix B for a list of participants and their affiliations.

[4] All of the papers are reproduced in Appendix D.

Each workshop was organized with a discussion leader and a recorder to take minutes. Participants had been provided with a list of questions pertinent to each topic and designed to focus workshop discussions.[5] Each three-hour discussion was tape recorded, and the recorders were charged with drafting a summary of the discussion and conclusions from each workshop for the planning committee. All leaders presented reports of the discussion and conclusions from their workshops at the final plenary session, held on Saturday afternoon.

Since the workshops constituted the heart of the conference and informed its findings and recommendations, a synopsis of the discussion and conclusions of each workshop are presented next. These summaries are derived from reports prepared by members of the planning committee who were present at particular workshops and who had access to minutes kept by assigned recorders as well as tape recordings of the discussions.

Workshops on
National Strategy for Documentation

The three workshops held concurrently on Friday afternoon addressed three main issues relating to a documentary strategy for immigrant records: collection development, preservation, and access.

COLLECTION DEVELOPMENT WORKSHOP

Issues Considered:
The members of this workshop considered several broad issues, including the changing definition of the term "ethnic" and the scope of ongoing efforts to collect immigrant/ethnic source materials. With regard to the latter, the group voiced concern that knowledge is lacking about the state of immigrant/ethnic archival collecting in both the United States and abroad. More specifically, the workshop participants dealt with the means to spur collection development and the need to consider a broader variety of immigrant/ethnic sources, including sources relating to new thematic areas such as sexuality, food, and street life, within the American ethnic experience.

---

[5] See Appendix A, the conference program, for names of workshop leaders and participants. See Appendix C for questions.

Discussion Highlights:

The recommendations of the workshop participants fell into three categories: broader guidelines for ethnic collection development, specific actions to be undertaken to support those guidelines, and long-term goals to be pursued by a variety of actions and projects.

The broader guidelines for collection development include the need to make repositories aware of the changing meanings of ethnicity and their relationship to ideas of race, class, and gender. In creating this awareness it should also be recognized that collections relating to different immigrant/ethnic groups are at varying developmental stages and, therefore, require different forms of assistance. Because of the limited resources now available to traditional (European-centered) immigrant/ethnic studies, many older collections have reached a plateau; and only passive collecting is underway. On the other hand, political and demographic changes are driving research interest in, but not necessarily archival collecting efforts for, recent immigrant groups. It is important, therefore, that attention be given equally to the records of both older and newer immigrant/ethnic groups.

In pursuing the wide spectrum of immigrant and ethnic sources, repositories should recognize that personal papers and other records of "insider perspective" have special value.

To foster better documentation of the American immigrant experience the workshop participants recommended specific immediate actions. These include the following:

1. A working group or steering committee should be created to continue the momentum of the planning conference (this was considered first priority). Eventually a central agency should be established to coordinate collection development initiatives, provide information, serve as a clearing house between American and foreign repositories, and take a centralized approach to funding sources when appropriate.

2. Second priority was to survey existing repositories at the collection level and create a regularly updated database of immigrant/ethnic records. The survey should build on existing directories, networks, and associations and include an analysis of current conditions of records. These actions were seen as absolutely necessary to understanding the current state of immigrant archives and to taking remedial or developmental action.

3. A long-term recommendation addressed the need to increase awareness on the part of immigrant/ethnic communities of the value of archival records, personal papers, and artifacts and to encourage them to take appropriate measures for their preservation. This could be done through a handbook, workshops, exhibits, and news releases. The development and upgrading of care of archival collections within ethnic communities could be encouraged by providing "archives extension" services in the form of professional consultation.

4. Another long-term goal recognized the great importance of the extensive American immigrant/ethnic sources in foreign repositories and the need to develop more effective modes of cooperation with repositories and colleagues in other countries, particularly to invite their collaboration in this project.

5. A third long-term goal is to identify those immigrant/ethnic communities, both old and new (e.g. Hmong, Cubans, Scotch-Irish) that are under- or undocumented and to take concerted action to develop archival collections.

PRESERVATION WORKSHOP

Issues Considered:
The working group on preservation discussed both the basic purpose of preserving immigrant-related materials and the specific means to accomplish preservation-related tasks, including the technologies to be applied, materials to be targeted for preservation, and the approaches to implementing both basic and more sophisticated preservation procedures.

Discussion Highlights:
The working group's consensus was that the primary purpose of preservation initiatives relating to immigrant source materials should be to preserve the information in those materials which are physically deteriorating or, by their nature, are in danger of deteriorating in the future. Selection for preservation treatment should be based on imminent danger of information loss.

The group's definition of preservation includes any technique that will engender a longer or, ideally, an archivally permanent life for immigrant-related materials. Therefore basic procedures such as the use of proper storage containers and provision of a correct storage environment are to be advocated as well as more complex techniques that involve the transfer of endangered material to stable media.

9

In the latter area, transfer to a stable preservation media, the group considered newer technologies but concluded that the use of archival microfilming remains the best means to preserve manuscript and print media.

Implementation of preservation work for immigrant-related materials can be accomplished through both education/advocacy, and wide scale, coordinated preservation work. Agencies holding immigrant-related materials need to be informed about the basic procedures that will result in an increased life span for their holdings. While most mainstream archival agencies appear to be aware of procedures such as the requirements for proper storage of archival collections, many organizations and individuals within ethnic communities who hold valuable collections are unfamiliar with such techniques. The group therefore advocated outreach programs such as workshops, distributing how-to-pamphlets, and articles in the immigrant/ethnic press that would help disseminate this information.

Secondly, the working group also advocated a coordinated effort directed at identifying and microfilming immigrant source materials that are in danger of deterioration and which have a broad scholarly utility. In making this recommendation, the role of the National Endowment for the Humanities-sponsored U.S. Newspaper Project in filming immigrant newspaper titles was recognized; indeed, the first step should be to encourage that project to include additional immigrant/ethnic publications. Any new microfilming initiative must certainly be coordinated with the U.S. Newspaper Project. Yet the group called for concerted action to identify and preserve other paper-based resources that are often unique to immigrant/ethnic groups. Such materials include, but are not limited to, almanacs and other serials (such as church and lodge newsletters), immigrant-press published books, and immigrant-related manuscript collections containing paper with a high degree of acidity.

In discussing preservation priorities, the working group also emphasized the importance of identifying non-textual immigrant-related material that pose special preservation problems. These include photographs, films, and sound recordings.

In order to carry out these objectives, the group agreed on the necessity of establishing an ongoing body concerned with the task of preserving immigrant-related source materials. This body should be composed of individuals with the necessary expertise to set standards for the selection of materials for preservation and to prescribe appropriate preservation methods; it could also serve as the coordinating body for dissemination of preservation-related information and the sponsoring agency for

10

workshops. The need for continuity in initiating and coordinating preservation of immigrant/ethnic materials was seen as the most critical of the working group's recommendations.

ACCESS WORKSHOP

Issues Considered:
The participants in this workshop considered one major issue, the best means of linking those who would use immigrant/ethnic source materials with those materials or with appropriate bibliographic data describing the sources. Explicit in the consideration of this issue was a definition of access and of the nature of immigrant/ethnic sources.

Discussion Highlights:
In considering the broad definitions concerning access and ethnic sources, the working group defined access as encompassing everything related to the process of connecting individual interests to available sources. The group determined that the number of people implied by the words "individual interests" is extensive and includes not only professional or academic researchers and archivists, but various members of society who want or need historical information on immigration or ethnicity for whatever reason. The group also recognized that this clientele consists both of people whose livelihood is directly associated with immigration history and those for whom immigration is a secondary or complementary component of research need.

In discussing the nature of immigrant/ethnic sources the workshop participants noted that the scope of such material is enormous. The interrelatedness of immigration history with other fields of inquiry and the great diversity of evidence available in repositories—many of them not specifically responsible for documenting immigration history—led to a discussion of trends in immigration historiography. It was noted that this greater awareness of the full spectrum of users and potential source material fosters an awareness of the broad context surrounding immigration and ethnicity. The group concluded that improvements in access to immigration-related materials could and would promote the significance of the immigration dimension for the study of other areas of American social history.

Compounding all considerations of access and source types was the group's uncertainty as to what materials—amidst the broad spectrum of ethnically-related sources—were available at what repositories.

Given these issues, the working group developed a series of specific action recommendations centered on the compilation and dissemination of descriptive information, the education of archivists and researchers, and the creation of a communication network between all who store, use, or are otherwise interested in ethnic sources. These action recommendations are:

1. the production of a single-volume guide to source material for the study of immigration and ethnicity; this is envisioned as a series of chapters, each of which would constitute an introduction to the major collections in the United States and other countries relating to a single immigrant/ethnic group. This initial volume would cover a range of the larger groups, but supplemental publications could in the future include smaller groups.

2. the development of a newsletter pertaining to the administration and use of historical documentation relating to immigration and ethnicity;

3. the promotion of the inclusion of immigration-related repositories and sources in major survey efforts and cataloging projects;

4. the occasional publication of special issues of the *Journal of American Ethnic History*, *Ethnic Forum*, or other publications devoted to available source material;

5. the creation of outreach tools, including perhaps video or other media, for acquainting records creators and custodians in ethnic communities with the research value and proper care of the sources they hold.

6. finally, the creation of an ongoing coalition or committee to carry out these specific initiatives.

Workshops on a Documentary History

The three workshops held concurrently on Saturday morning addressed the three main issues relating to the documentary history project: content definition, format definition, and administration.

CONTENT DEFINITION WORKSHOP

Issues Considered:
The members of the content definition workshop considered four major issues relating to the content of a documentary history of the immigrant experience. These were the purpose of and audience for such a documentary history; the chronological and ethnic parameters of the series; the common themes to be considered within each documentary history; and the types of documents to be used as well as the criteria for their selection.

Discussion Highlights:
Members of the workshop concluded that the documentary histories should serve a broad audience of scholars, students and lay readers. To achieve this goal the project might issue each volume in several formats. A full-format volume with an accompanying microfilm edition of original documents could serve the scholarly community. An abridged paperback version of each volume might then be produced for a more general readership. In both the full and abridged volumes, translations would be provided for original documents so as to enhance their utility for non-specialist scholars and lay readers. The microfilm addendum to the full volume would permit scholars with ethnic specialization to more closely examine original sources in their original languages.

The project would encompass the American immigrant experience from the sixteenth century to the present and would consider all immigrant/ethnic groups not now being treated by other documentary projects. Given this inclusive character, the members of the workshop recommended that the initial volumes of the series deal with immigrant/ethnic communities for which there are sufficient documentary resources currently available but that the groups selected also reflect a broad continental/chronological spectrum; e.g., groups from Asia, Eastern Europe, Western Europe, and the Western Hemisphere might comprise the first project components.

Thematically, the volumes should reflect the internal life of the immigrant groups and the dynamic quality of the immigrant experience, noting changes that took place in the lives of individuals before, during, and after the migration process. Among the issues to be considered would be occupation, religion, politics, education, return migration, child-rearing practices, generational conflict, intra-group conflict, and class differences. Gender should be given special emphasis when dealing with these topics. The documents selected for each volume should preferably be those that permit the immigrant to speak in his or her own voice rather than outside sources commenting on the immigrant experience.

Documents selected for publication should be both traditional—letters, diaries, etc.—and non-traditional—photographs, sound recordings, art work, etc. For non-text formats the project might consider issuing videotapes and sound recordings. In the selection of documents, preference should be given to materials that have not been previously published.

FORMAT DEFINITION WORKSHOP

Issues Considered:
Members of this workshop considered whether a documentary history of immigration should be issued in a series of thematic or ethnic-specific volumes and whether the documents selected for those volumes should go beyond traditional textual sources. The workshop participants also discussed the audience for this documentary publication and the general mission of the project.

Discussion Highlights:
In reviewing the general purpose of the documentary project the workshop members recommended that the series be viewed as a tool to encourage development of scholarship in the field of immigration history (the series should not be treated as definitive statements of history), as a means to evoke interest in history and documentary preservation on the part of ethnic communities, as a resource to assist in the development of curricula at college levels, and as a means to encourage communication of ideas about immigration to the broader public.

Given these assumptions, the workshop participants concluded that the series should consist of volumes structured around the history and experiences of specific immigrant/ethnic groups. Each volume would include an introductory history of the group, documentary reproductions, and bibliographical essays. Some standard categories should be covered in each volume, including topics such as religion, work, family, etc. It was recognized, however, that a considerable margin of individuality needs to be retained within each volume to accommodate characteristics peculiar to particular ethnic groups.

ADMINISTRATION WORKSHOP

Issues Considered:
The chief issues discussed at this workshop were the structure of an administrative entity responsible for carrying out the documentary history project and the functions that body would perform.

Discussion Highlights

The scope, character, and structure of a central entity that would have national responsibility for the administration of the documentary history project could not be decided within the context of the conference. Nor could the relationship between the archival projects stemming from a national strategy for documenting the immigrant experience and the documentary history project be defined in any specific form. Yet there was general agreement regarding the need for some kind of central entity that would have oversight over both components. Various alternative models were discussed, but no one was fixed upon.

The recommendations of the administration workshop therefore are of a general nature and do not pretend to offer a definitive blueprint for the central entity.

The documentary history project should be administered by one legal entity able to receive and award monies and sign contracts. This body would have a small staff responsible to a board composed of archivists, historians, documentary editors, and other individuals with an interest in the goals of the project. Nine basic functions are envisioned for this entity:

1. planning the entire project;
2. fund raising for endowment and current support;
3. identifying and selecting each component volume and its editor;
4. monitoring the progress of each volume;
5. negotiating and executing all publication contracts;
6. accounting for all national project monies;
7. assisting in marketing project products;
8. maintaining communication with the project's constituencies in the United States and abroad;
9. undertaking an initial survey of immigrant/ethnics sources in repositories in the United States and, insofar as possible, abroad, and publishing the findings.

The central entity would have at least three standing committees: fund raising and promotion, selection of editors and volumes, and project oversight. A small staff would carry out the work of the central entity including administrative and budgetary functions and conducting the initial survey of immigrant/ethnic-related resources. The results of this survey would be published in volume form no later than two years after the project was initiated.

Each project component (documentary volume) would be directed by an editor working with a team of research assistants, translators, and archivists as needed. He/she would have the counsel of a small editorial advisory

15

board composed of scholars (including specialists in and representatives of the culture being treated) and fund raisers. While major funding would be provided by the central entity, each project component would be expected to raise a significant amount of funding. In conjunction with the production of the documentary volume each project would necessarily undertake a detailed survey of sources pertinent to the volume.

Each director/editor would be responsible for designing the individual project volume. Once the design and funding arrangements of the individual documentary project had been approved by the central entity, the director, staff and advisory board of the project would be fully responsible for carrying out the work. Liaison with and oversight of the component projects would be maintained by the staff and board of the central entity, which would assist with fund raising and coordination with other specific projects.

The board and staff of the central entity, as well as the director/editor, staff, and advisory editorial committee for each specific project, would require institutional homes, presumably universities or other research institutions. The host institution would be expected to provide some support for the segment of the project that it sheltered. In addition, the overall project would have to raise considerable monies.

The central entity would coordinate fund raising efforts, which would be carried out at the national level by its board and staff; in addition, the fund raising by the editor/director, staff, and editorial board of each project would be subject to coordination by the central entity. A variety of funding sources were discussed. Public and private foundations, businesses, ethnic organizations and individuals in the United States and abroad, foreign governments, and congressional appropriations were some of the possible sources identified. The development of an endowment and the employment of professional fund raisers were also considered, as was utilizing the expertise and resources developed through the fund raising efforts associated with the Statue of Liberty and Ellis Island restoration projects. Proceeds from publications would, of course, also be reinvested in the project.

Final Plenary and Postconference Work

At the closing plenary session on Saturday afternoon, reports from the workshops were presented, followed by an open discussion of the main findings and recommendations that had emerged from two days of intensive exchanges of ideas. While no formal polling of opinion took place, an impressive degree of consensus emerged from this final discussion. The Agenda for Action below reflects this consensus.

A major topic of discussion at the plenary was definition of the scope of a project to document the immigrant experience. Diverse opinions were expressed, but it was agreed that the focus should be on the immigrant experience broadly defined. The concept of immigration encompasses a variety of experiences, including those of sojourners, refugees, permanent migrants, indentured servants, and slaves. In addition to issues of background causes and processes of migration, the agenda should extend to development of ethnic identities and cultures in the new country, as manifested not only among the immigrants but in subsequent generations.

The conference planning committee was formally charged by the final plenary session with developing and issuing the conference report and seeking to implement its recommendations. Following the conference, tapes of proceedings were transcribed and notes kept by reporters compiled and distributed to members of the planning committee. At a meeting held January 10-12, 1991, in Washington, D.C., the committee reviewed and synthesized the workshop reports and conference recommendations into an initial draft of the report. Subsequently individual members drafted various sections of the national strategy statement.

Reconstituting itself as the Project to Document the Immigrant Experience, the committee met again March 8-10, 1991 to complete work on a version of the document, which was then sent to all conference participants for further suggestions. In addition, the PDIE planning committee applied for and received a supplemental grant from NHPRC to publish and distribute this report. It is also preparing a proposal for a one-year development grant that would provide for detailed planning and initial implementation of several of the specific projects recommended by the conference.

17

AGENDA FOR ACTION

The Agenda for Action that follows states in concise language the major recommendations for specific projects that emerged from this process and that comprise the essential components of the Project to Document the Immigrant Experience, a national strategy for documenting immigration and ethnicity in the United States.

1. **Establish an ongoing administrative entity to plan, coordinate, promote, and raise funds for projects aimed at addressing needs identified in the conference.**

The question of implementation of the conference's various recommendations was a recurring item in presentations and discussions. CDIE participants stressed the necessity for some type of central organization to plan and execute the interrelated series of projects and to sustain the momentum of interest and cooperation sparked by the conference. The scope and character of this central entity were not defined. Some conferees suggested forming a "coalition" of existing archival or historical institutions; while others favored a newly constituted commission or group comprised of historians, archivists, fund raisers, editors, ethnic community representatives, and others connected with preserving and promoting the documentary heritage of American immigration. As a first step toward establishing a central body, the conference planning committee was charged by the conferees with serving in a coordinating capacity during the formation of initial projects. This group will be known as the Project on Documenting the Immigrant Experience (PDIE) committee.

2. **Develop a newsletter for historians, archivists, and others significantly involved in the custody or use of documentation of the immigrant/ethnic experience.**

Participants repeatedly affirmed the value of sustaining and expanding the communication network established by the conference. To begin addressing this need, the conference proposed that a newsletter pertaining to the collection, preservation, use, and publication of primary sources on immigration be published. Many details surrounding the content and production of this circular are yet to be determined, but it will have the overall objective of facilitating collaboration through information sharing among conference participants and other interested parties.

3. Compile and disseminate information about source material for research in immigration/ethnic history.

CDIE conferees commented on the current lack of guides or other reference tools describing immigrant/ethnic documentation. The need exists both for reporting of source material for various immigrant/ethnic groups and for more detailed listings of holdings for individual repositories. The conferees proposed the publication of a single-volume compendium of essays outlining the scope and value of primary sources for a selected number of immigrant/ethnic groups. This guide will serve as an effective introduction to documentary sources for researchers, students, and archivists. It will enhance planning efforts for further collaborative projects and furnish a useful starting point for more comprehensive and refined survey and description efforts.

4. Promote and develop initiatives to collect/accession new source materials, particularly those that address poorly documented ethnic groups or other neglected dimensions of American immigration.

Conferees concurred that much remains to be done in gathering immigrant/ethnic documentation now in private custody and often in danger of destruction. Although some immigrant/ethnic groups are better documented than others, no group can claim to have anything approaching a complete record; for some groups, this process has barely begun. Through a newsletter, other outreach efforts, and eventually multi-institutional acquisition projects, consciousness of these needs can be raised and new collaborative collecting initiatives taken.

5. Initiate new projects and promote existing efforts to arrange, describe, and preserve immigrant documentation.

Conferees agreed that no archival institution has sufficient resources for processing and preserving its collections to ideal standards. In even the best endowed repositories of immigrant/ethnic documentation, important material remains inaccessible because it is either unorganized, inadequately described, or in fragile physical condition; in less well funded repositories, the situation is much worse. This problem should be addressed at the multi-institutional levels through coordinated fund raising and sharing of expertise and resources. Ongoing projects (e.g., the National Inventory of

Documentary Sources sponsored by Chadwyck-Healey, the NEH U.S. Newspaper Project, and the consortia-based cataloging and preservation work of groups like Research Libraries Group and Online Computer Library Center) should be encouraged to incorporate immigrant/ethnic source materials. As an initial project the survey and microfilming of immigrant/ethnic serials (which are not included in the NEH U.S. Newspaper Project and which are often at risk) is recommended.

6. Develop outreach programs to ethnic archives and historical organizations, and ethnic communities generally, to increase awareness of the value of, and assist them in the proper care of, historical documentation.

Conferees agreed that the success of a national program dealing with immigrant/ethnic documentation depends heavily upon the involvement of the immigrant/ethnic communities themselves. A substantial portion of valuable material is in the custody of the historical societies, fraternal organization archives, museums, libraries, and other institutions of those communities. The participation of these and other organizations should be enlisted through a variety of means including workshops, media presentations, news articles, and public presentations. One of the early initiatives should be a conference of ethnic historical organizations and institutions. Most of these activities should focus on the importance of historical records and the ways in which they can best be preserved. Such outreach programs should be coordinated with the Society of American Archivists, the American Association for State and Local History, and others who have undertaken similar initiatives.

7. Produce a multi-volume, multi-media series of documentary editions on the immigrant experience

The conferees endorsed the production of a documentary history of immigration. Such a documentary history would be, in a sense, the culminating outcome of the archival work of collection and preservation. It would enable the immigrants to speak in their own voices to a larger public. The conferees noted that this project would, of necessity, be costly, long term, and require careful planning. A great many complex issues must be resolved in advance of launching the first volume in this series. Specific plans (based on general conference recommendations) must be made for the content, format, and administration of the series as a whole and of individual volumes.

CONFERENCE ON DOCUMENTING THE IMMIGRANT EXPERIENCE

November 15-17, 1990

IDS Oak Ridge Conference Center
Chaska, Minnesota

Sponsored by the History Committee
Statue of Liberty-Ellis Island Foundation

Administered by
Immigration History Research Center
University of Minnesota

PROGRAM

THURSDAY EVENING, November 15

6:00- 7:30 Reception, Buffet Supper

7:30- 9:00 Plenary: Opening Session
Room 208

Papers:

Rudolph J. Vecoli
"Why a Conference on Documenting the Immigrant Experience?"

John Grabowski
"Archivists and Immigrants, Embarking for New Destinations Together"

FRIDAY MORNING, November 16

Breakfast
(served beginning at 7:00 a.m.)

8:30-10:00 PLENARY SESSION: A National Strategy for Documentation
Room 208

Papers:

Joel Wurl
"The Archival Golden Door: Thoughts on Improving the State of Historical Documentation on the Immigrant Experience"

Kathleen Neils Conzen
"Hunting the Snark; or, The Historian's Quest for Immigrant Documentation"

10:00-10:15 Refreshment Break

10:15-11:45 PLENARY SESSION: A Documentary
History
Room 208

Papers:

Alan Kraut
*"In Their Own Words: Why Historians
Need a Documentary History of the
Immigrant Experience"*

Mary Lynn McCree Bryan
*"Voice for the Voiceless:
A Means to an End"*

11:45- 1:00 Lunch

FRIDAY AFTERNOON, November 16

1:00- 4:00 Concurrent Working Groups:
A National Strategy for Documentation

(2:30- 2:45 Refreshment Break)

I) <u>Collection Development</u> Room 201

R. Joseph Anderson, Moderator
Mary Lynn McCree Bryan
Roy Bryce-Laporte
John Fleckner
Ronald Grele
Dirk Hoerder
Kerby Miller
Nélida Pérez
George Pozzetta
Gianfausto Rosoli
Leo Schelbert
Maxine Seller
Rudolph Vecoli
L. Ling-chi Wang

Concurrent Working Groups:
A National Strategy for Documentation
(continued)

II) Preservation Room 203

George Tselos, Moderator
James Danky
Candace Falk
John Grabowski
James Grossman
Laura Gutiérrez-Witt
Yuji Ichioka
Alan Kraut
Odd Lovoll
Thaddeus Radzilowski
Albert Tezla
Marek Web
Elisabeth Wittman
Virginia Yans-McLaughlin

III) Access Room 205

David Klaassen, Moderator
Dag Blanck
Albert Camarillo
Kathleen Neils Conzen
Jay Dolan
Kenneth Fones-Wolf
A. William Hoglund
Franklin Odo
Moses Rischin
Gabrielle Scardellato
Robert Shuster
Lydio Tomasi
Joel Wurl
Lubomyr Wynar

5:00   Cash Bar

6:00   Dinner

8:00   Film Program
        Room 208

Breakfast
(served beginning at 7:00 a.m.)

8:30-11:30 Concurrent Working Groups:
A Documentary History

(10:00-10:15 Refreshment Break)

IV) Content Definition Room 201

Maxine Seller, Moderator
Dag Blanck
Kathleen Neils Conzen
Jay Dolan
John Grabowski
Yuji Ichioka
Alan Kraut
Odd Lovoll
Gabrielle Scardellato
Lydio Tomasi
George Tselos
Marek Web
Elisabeth Wittman
Virginia Yans-McLaughlin

V) Format Definition Room 203

Franklin Odo, Moderator
R. Joseph Anderson
Roy Bryce-Laporte
James Danky
John Fleckner
Kenneth Fones-Wolf
A. William Hoglund
David Klaassen
Nélida Pérez
George Pozzetta
Moses Rischin
Gianfausto Rosoli
Albert Tezla
Lubomyr Wynar

Concurrent Working Groups:
A Documentary History
(continued)

VI) Project Administration   **Room 205**

Candace Falk, Moderator
Mary Lynn McCree Bryan
Albert Camarillo
Ronald Grele
James Grossman
Laura Gutiérrez-Witt
Dirk Hoerder
Kerby Miller
Thaddeus Radzilowski
Leo Schelbert
Robert Shuster
Rudolph Vecoli
L. Ling-chi Wang
Joel Wurl

11:30- 1:00 Lunch

SATURDAY AFTERNOON, NOVEMBER 17

1:00- 4:30 PLENARY: Closing Session   **Room 208**

Reports from Working Groups

2:30-2:45 Refreshment Break

Formulation of Recommendations

4:30   Adjourn

5:00   Departure by bus for IHRC

6:00   Reception at the IHRC

Shuttle bus to Days Inn Hotel

The Conference on Documenting the Immigrant Experience has been funded by a grant from the Statue of Liberty-Ellis Island Foundation to its History Committee and a matching grant from the National Historical Publications and Records Commission.

Members of the History Committee, Statue of Liberty-Ellis Island Foundation

Kathleen Neils Conzen
Department of History, University of Chicago

Roger Daniels
Department of History, University of Cincinnati

Jay Dolan
Director, Cushwa Center for the Study of American Catholicism, University of Notre Dame

Victor Greene
Department of History, University of Wisconsin-Milwaukee

F. Ross Holland, Jr.
Independent Historian

Louise Año Nuevo Kerr
Associate Vice Chancellor for Academic Affairs, University of Illinois-Chicago

Alan Kraut
Department of History, American University

Bara Levin
Archivist

Dwight Pitcaithly
Regional Historian, National Park Service

Moses Rischin
Department of History, San Francisco State University

Rudolph Vecoli, Chair
Director, Immigration History Research Center, and Department of History, University of Minnesota

Virginia Yans-McLaughlin
Department of History, Rutgers University

Conference Planning Committee

R. Joseph Anderson
Library Director, The Balch Institute

Mary Lynn McCree Bryan
Editor, The Jane Addams Papers, Duke University

John Grabowski
Curator of Manuscripts, The Western Reserve Historical Society

Alan Kraut
Department of History, American University

Franklin Odo
Director, Ethnic Studies Program, University of Hawaii at Manoa

Rudolph Vecoli
Director, Immigration History Research Center, and Department of History, University of Minnesota

Joel Wurl
Curator, Immigration History Research Center, University of Minnesota

The Conference on Documenting the Immigrant Experience has a two-fold purpose:

1. to devise a collective strategy for preservation, collection development, and access to materials for immigration history research by bringing together those who gather and keep the archives and those who use them, along with representatives of publishers and funding agencies.

2. to explore the feasibility of publishing a series of volumes to document the history of immigrant groups through their own writings on the immigrant experience.

Appendix B — Participants and Observers

Joseph Anderson
Library Director
The Balch Institute
Philadelphia, Pennsylvania

Prof. Dag Blanck
Centre for Multiethnic Research
Uppsala University, Sweden
and Director, Swenson Swedish
American Research Center,
Augustana College
Rock Island, Illinois

Mary Lynn McCree Bryan
Editor, Jane Addams Papers
Duke University
Fayetteville, North Carolina

Prof. Roy S. Bryce-Laporte
Director, Africana and Hispanic
Studies Program
Colgate University
Hamilton, New York

Prof. Albert Camarillo
Department of History
Stanford University
Stanford, California

Prof. Kathleen Neils Conzen
Department of History
University of Chicago
Chicago, Illinois

James Danky
Librarian,
State Historical Society of
Wisconsin
Madison, Wisconsin

Prof. Jay P. Dolan, Director
Cushwa Center for the Study of
American Catholicism
University of Notre Dame
Notre Dame, Indiana

Candace Falk
Editor, Emma Goldman Papers
University of California
Berkeley, California

John Fleckner
Archives Center
Museum of American History
Smithsonian Institution
Washington, D.C.

Prof. Kenneth Fones-Wolf
History Department
West Virginia University
and West Virginia and Regional
History Collection
Morgantown, West Virginia

John Grabowski
Curator of Manuscripts
The Western Reserve Historical
Society
Cleveland, Ohio

Dr. Ronald Grele
Oral History Research Office
Columbia University
New York, New York

James Grossman
Director, Family and
Community History Program
Newberry Library
Chicago, Illinois

Laura Gutiérrez-Witt
Curator, Benson Latin American
Collection
University of Texas
Austin, Texas

Prof. Dirk Hoerder
Department of History
University of Bremen
Bremen, Germany

Prof. A. William Hoglund
Department of History
University of Connecticut
Storrs, Connecticut

Prof. Yuji Ichioka
Asian American Studies Center
University of California-Los
  Angeles
Los Angeles, California

David Klaassen
Director, Social Welfare History
Archives
University of Minnesota
Minneapolis, Minnesota

Prof. Alan Kraut
Department of History
The American University
Washington, D.C.

Prof. Odd Lovoll
Norwegian American Historial
  Association
St. Olaf College
Northfield, Minnesota

Prof. Kerby A. Miller
Department of History
University of Missouri
Columbia, Missouri

Prof. Franklin Odo
Director, Ethnic Studies Program
University of Hawaii-Manoa
Honolulu, Hawaii

Nélida Pérez
Librarian and Archivist
Center for Puerto Rican Studies
Hunter College
New York, New York

Prof. George Pozzetta
Department of History
University of Florida
Gainesville, Florida

Prof. Thaddeus Radzilowski
Department of History
Southwest State University
Marshall, Minnesota

Prof. Moses Rischin
Department of History
San Francisco State University
San Francisco, California

Gianfausto Rosoli
Director, Centro Studi
  Emigrazione
Rome, Italy

Gabrielle Scardellato
Multicultural History Society of
  Ontario
Toronto, Ontario

Prof. Leo Schelbert
Department of History
University of Illinois-Chicago
Chicago, Illinois

Prof. Maxine S. Seller
Graduate School of Education
SUNY-Buffalo
Buffalo, New York

Robert Shuster
Director of Archives
Billy Graham Center
Wheaton College
Wheaton, Illinois

Prof. Emeritus Albert Tezla
Department of English
University of Minnesota-Duluth
Duluth, Minnesota
(documentary editor, Hungarian
  Americans)

Prof. Lydio Tomasi
Executive Director
Center for Migration Studies
Staten Island, New York

George Tselos
(coordinator, Greek American
  Archives Project)
Archivist
Edison National Historic Site
West Orange, New Jersey

Prof. Rudolph J. Vecoli
Director, Immigration History
  Research Center
University of Minnesota
St. Paul, Minnesota

Prof. L. Ling-chi Wang
Chair, Department of Ethnic
  Studies
Asian American Studies
  Program
University of California-Berkeley
Berkeley, California

Marek Web
Curator, YIVO Institute for
  Jewish Research
New York, New York

Elizabeth Wittman
Chief Archivist, Evang. Lutheran
  Church in America Archives
Chicago, Illinois

Joel Wurl
Curator, Immigration History
  Research Center
University of Minnesota
St. Paul, Minnesota

Prof. Lubomyr R. Wynar
Center for the Study of Ethnic
  Publ. and Cultural Inst.
Kent State University
Kent, Ohio

Prof. Virginia Yans-McLaughlin
Department of History
Rutgers University
New Brunswick, New Jersey

Observers

Randy Boehm
University Publications of
  America
Bethesda, Maryland

Roger Bruns
Publications Program
National Historical Publications
  and Records Commission
National Archives
Washington, D.C.

George Farr
Director, Office of Preservation
National Endowment for the
  Humanities
Washington, D.C.

Cynthia Harris
Executive Editor
Greenwood Press
Westport, Connecticut

Barry Katzen
Director
Kraus International Publications
Millwood, New York

Nancy Sahli
Director, Records Program
National Historical Publications
  and Records Commission
National Archives
Washington, D.C.

Susan Severtson
Chadwyck-Healey Inc.
Alexandria, Virginia

Richard Wentworth
Director
University of Illinois Press
Champaign, Illinois

Appendix C — Questions Addressed at Workshops

WORKSHOPS—A NATIONAL STRATEGY FOR DOCUMENTATION

I. COLLECTION DEVELOPMENT - Joseph Anderson, Moderator

1. What kinds of institutions and repositories acquire or maintain source material for the study of immigration history?

2. Are repositories active enough in collecting ethnic/immigration material? Have you seen change in the level of activity over time? If so, what accounts for this?

3. How can collecting be encouraged and facilitated?

4. Should collection development activity be coordinated among various repositories? What is to be gained by moving in this direction? What are the potential drawbacks?

5. If multi-institutional coordination is desirable, how can this be accomplished? What is needed in the way of resources? communication mechanisms?

6. What roles do/should ethnic communities or institutions play in developing research collections?

7. What, if any, existing models of successful collection building can be emulated?

8. How can the perspectives and insights of researchers best be incorporated in collection development; i.e., how can archivists/librarians be most responsive to the needs of researchers and vice versa? How can researchers actively participate in the process?

9. How completely is the immigrant experience currently documented in archives and libraries? What are the major strengths? What are the gaps?

10. What types of sources—traditional printed or manuscript material as well as audiovisual or other less traditional media—are generally most valuable in documenting the immigrant experience?

11. How can efforts to improve collection development take into account pertinent documentation and projects in countries of emigration?

12. How can collection development efforts take into account relevant documentation in government archives, state historical societies, local libraries, and other repositories whose missions are not devoted exclusively to the immigrant experience?

II. PRESERVATION - George Tselos, Moderator

1. What types of sources—traditional printed or manuscript material as well as audiovisual or other less traditional media—are generally most valuable in documenting the immigrant experience?

2. What types of source material related to immigration command the highest priority for preservation work? How do perspectives of scholars, archivists, and ethnic communities compare on this issue?

3. What preservation efforts and technologies currently exist that might be emulated or adopted by repositories of immigration material?

4. Can preservation efforts be coordinated among various archives and libraries? Are there useful models of such coordinated or consortium-based projects?

5. What are some of the most pressing, serious problems regarding the current condition of immigrant documentation?

6. What role can historians and other researchers play in ensuring the preservation of archival and library material?

7. What kinds of short-term, immediate actions can be undertaken to begin addressing preservation problems? What respective roles can be played by researchers, archivists, and ethnic communities?

8. What kinds of long-term strategies can be identified for improving the condition of immigrant documentation? What is required in the way of resources in order to accomplish these objectives, and from where can these resources be obtained? To what extent can/should funding be sought from within ethnic communities?

III. ACCESS - Dave Klaassen, Moderator

1. What problems currently exist in obtaining sufficient information about the location and content of immigrant documentation?

2. Who are the primary users of immigration-related documentation? How can efforts to improve access address different needs/interests of these user groups?

3. What kinds of access-related opportunities or technologies currently exist that could be adopted by immigration repositories?

4. What have repositories with immigrant material done thus far to make material accessible? What kinds of descriptive guides/tools are available for researchers, at the single institution and multi-institution levels? Are these products useful? Are they used?

5. How do researchers of immigration-related topics learn of relevant material? Are these methods adequate for identifying the most useful documentation?

6. How can efforts to improve research access best incorporate material in non-US repositories?

7. How can researchers, archivists, and librarians communicate more systematically regarding the availability of documentation and its research value?

8. To what extent does language translation play a role in making immigration sources fully accessible?

9. How can efforts to improve research access best incorporate material located in institutions that are not sufficiently staffed or routinely open for research use?

10. What kinds of access restrictions or limitations are prevalent in dealing with immigration material? To what extent are these restrictions hindering research efforts?

11. What do researchers encounter in archival institutions in the way of services and facilities? What are some of the most and least preferable features of archival research environments?

35

WORKSHOPS—A DOCUMENTARY HISTORY

IV. CONTENT DEFINITION - Maxine Seller, Moderator

1. What is the purpose of a documentary publication series on the immigrant experience?

2. What is the intended audience for this documentary series? Would the editions be developed in such a way as to serve the needs of researchers outside the field of history? How can this be accomplished?

3. How is the "immigrant experience" to be defined for this publication project? Will the series encompass, for example, the experiences of the children of immigrants or the persistence of ethnicity after the primary era of immigration?

4. Which immigrant groups should be represented in a documentary history series. What rationale can be applied in making this decision?

5. What time period should be covered? Rationale?

6. What aspects of the immigrant experience should be focused upon in a documentary history; i.e., should the volumes include <u>only</u> documents produced by the immigrants themselves? Should they include material on pre-immigration forces/backgrounds?

7. How can the project ensure that the editions will cover a wide range of experiences, cutting across gender, social class, and region of settlement?

8. Should a documentary series incorporate important "non-textual" sources, such as music, art, photographs? How can this be accomplished?

9. How will non-English-language material be incorporated? Will translations be provided for such documents? If so, would the original-language version be included as well?

10. What kinds of factors will govern the selection of documents to be included in volumes? How inclusive or restrictive should the criteria be?

11. Should the series be organized by ethnic group (i.e., separate volumes for Poles, Chinese, Germans, etc.) or thematically? How should material be organized within each volume?

V. FORMAT DEFINITION - Franklin Odo, Moderator

1. To what extent will the volumes be annotated? What purpose will the annotations serve?

2. Should the series be organized by ethnic group (i.e., separate volumes for Poles, Chinese, Germans, etc.) or thematically? How should material be organized within each volume?

3. Should the editions be made available in microform? compact or laser disc? hard copy only? a combination of these?

4. Should the volumes include illustrations? indexes? bibliographies? How extensive should these components be?

5. What kind of information should be included in the introductory sections of each volume? Should there be, for example, an overview of the history of the particular ethnic group or theme being documented?

6. How much standardization/consistency will be applied to every volume in the series; i.e., will each volume address a standard list of themes and follow a set framework for ordering the chapters and the documents within the chapters?

7. If translations are to be provided, how/where will these appear in the volumes?

8. Are there model documentary editions that could be emulated? What are the appealing features of these publications?

9. Should a documentary series incorporate important "non-textual" sources, such as music, art, photographs? How can this be accomplished?

10. How can the project ensure that the editions will cover a wide range of experiences, cutting across gender, social class, and region of settlement?

VI. PROJECT ADMINISTRATION - Candace Falk, Moderator

1. How should the project be organized overall, administratively and as to funding?

2. How should editorial responsibility be assigned for a) individual volumes; b) the overall series? Will there be an editorial board? a single managing editor? an editorial board and/or single editor for each volume?

3. What is needed in the way of support staff for producing each volume?

4. Where should the project be based? What kinds of facilities or arrangements are required of the institution that serves in this capacity?

5. What amount of funding will be required to produce volumes? How can such funds best be raised?

6. Presuming there are adequate resources, what would constitute a reasonable timetable for producing individual volumes?

7. If translations are to be provided, how will this activity be administered, and what effect will this have on scheduling and expenses?

8. How will the documents themselves be located, selected, and accumulated?

9. What are the first steps required in getting this project underway?

10. How can the project ensure that the editions will cover a wide range of experiences, cutting across gender, social class, and region of settlement?

11. What, overall, are the key ingredients to achieving a successful documentary publication project?

Why a Conference on Documenting the Immigrant Experience?

Rudolph J. Vecoli

Let me begin by acknowledging the indispensable support of the Statue of Liberty/Ellis Island Foundation and the National Historical Publications and Records Commission. Matching grants from these agencies have made this conference possible. Behind institutions, even funding agencies, are individuals. I particularly want to express our appreciation to Stephen J. Briganti, President and CEO of the Statue of Liberty/Ellis Island Foundation for his support of the role of the History Committee and of this project in particular. Similarly, I thank Mary Giunta, Acting Director, Publications Program, NHPRC, and Nancy Sahli, Director, Records Program, NHPRC, for their encouragement of and enthusiasm for this undertaking.

The immediate stimulus for this conference came from the History Committee of the Statue of Liberty/Ellis Island Centennial Commission. Established in 1983, the committee met periodically over a period of seven years to provide advice with respect to issues of historical preservation and interpretation relating to these historic sites. The committee members[1]— most of whom are here today—believed that the centennials of the Statue of Liberty and Ellis Island, in addition to securing the physical restoration of these monuments, should serve the purpose of advancing scholarly and popular understanding of the significance of immigration in American history. We therefore initiated several projects, including the Statue of Liberty/Ellis Island Centennial Series, published by the University of Illinois Press,[2] a symposium on the occasion of the 100th anniversary of the statue,[3] and an atlas of American immigration history. The idea of a documentary history of American immigration aroused particular ethusiasm among members of the committee. Several members of the committee, Victor Greene, Alan Kraut, and Bara Levin, invested a great deal of effort in developing this idea and preparing a prospectus. This conference is really the fruit of their initial spadework.

Although the Statue of Liberty/Ellis Island Foundation has been rather singleminded in its concentration on the bricks-and-mortar mission of physicial restoration, it agreed to fund several of the History Committee's projects, including a conference to consider the feasibility of a documentary history of American immigration. Meanwhile, the idea of a documentary project in immigration history had emerged independently from the discussions of the National Historical Publications and Records Commission. Once we discovered we were thinking along the same lines, it was a foregone conclusion that we would join forces.

As we continued our discussions it became clear to the History Committee as well as to NHPRC that a documentary history project could only be considered within the larger context of the state of documentation respecting the immigrant experience. Hence the two-pronged character of this conference agenda. One objective is to address the matter of a national strategy for documentation; a second objective is to consider the desirability and feasibility of the compilation and publication of a documentary history of American immigration. Given the complexity of these matters, it followed that the conference participants should represent a variety of backgrounds, experiences, and disciplines. That is why you are here.

At the risk of repeating myself, let me say that this is a working conference. This is reflected in the format of the conference: most of our time will be spent in the working groups, which have been assigned quite specific tasks. Within the broad parameters that the deliberations will address immigration into the United States from throughout the world in the 19th and 20th centuries, the outcomes of the conference will be determined by you. We seek your answers to the questions that have been posed; beyond that we anticipate that from the collective wisdom of this assembly will come proposals of a practical and specific nature for realizing our objectives. For this reason, Saturday afternoon has been reserved for a plenary session at which reports from the working groups will be presented and recommendations formulated.

On the basis of the conference discussions and recommendations, the planning committee will prepare a report for nationwide distribution. The committee may also generate proposals for particular projects, if that appears appropriate. We expect, moreover, that the report will stimulate scholars and institutions around the country to undertake innovative projects. Our purpose in sum is to serve as a catalyst to generate fresh thinking, energy, and enthusiasm with respect to the documentation of the history of immigration into the United States.

Having described the immediate circumstances that have brought us together, allow me to share with you some reflections on the larger context of our meeting: the underlying intellectual, political, and social developments that have made the subject of immigration once again a matter of moment. As you know, the Ellis Island Museum of Immigration was inaugurated on September 9, 1990. The culmination of a decades-long effort to preserve this historic monument, it represents the triumph of memory over amnesia. You will recall that following its closing as an immigration station in 1954, the federal government sought to sell off Ellis Island to the highest bidder; no one at the time appeared to be concerned with its historic significance. The campaign to preserve Ellis Island as a historical monument to our immigrant forebears is itself a complicated, problematic story.[4] Suffice it to say that the establishment of the Museum of Immigration symbolizes a basic shift in historical paradigms. The theme of immigration has moved from the periphery to center stage in American history. From the marginal man, the immigrant has been transformed into the archetypal American. As a people we have increasingly. come to interpret ourselves through the medium of the immigrant experience. How and why this came about is a matter of conjecture. The ethnic revival, the "roots" phenomenon, and the dramatic increase in immigration of the past two decades, all, I suggest, contributed to this reconstruction of the American narrative.[5]

This development is a part of a larger historical reconstruction which has replaced the consensus paradigm with an emphasis on diversity and conflict as emblematic of the American past. Rejecting the assimilationist symbol of the Melting Pot, Americans have generally espoused a pluralist vision of their society, one in which multiculturalism is a dominant motif. Elements which had been absent or silent in traditional history texts, women, workers, ethnic/racial groups, and immigrants, are now viewed as historical actors, struggling to control their own lives. The "new social history," has been both a mirror of the changes in contemporary society and an agent of change in thinking about that society.

Because of these changes, our educational system, from elementary schools through the universities, is confronted today with the challenge of providing multicultural education to its students. While definitions vary, at a minimum multicultural education must, I propose, convey understanding about and sensitivity to the differences among people which stem from diversity of language, religion, culture, race, and gender. Surely immigration which has been and continues to be a major source of such differences must be a major theme in any multicultural curriculum. Yet my impression is that much which currently passes for multicultural education is grossly deficient in dealing with the history of immigration. This presents a particular challenge to those of us who, as historians, archivists, administrators, program officers, and publishers, are concerned with the creation and dissemination of historical scholarship. This is the larger challenge to which, I believe, this conference is responding. The question, "how do we document the immigrant experience?," carries within it the broader query: how can we broaden and deepen our understanding of the manner in which immigration has shaped the multicultural character of American society?

The idea of documenting the immigrant experience is certainly not new. Marcus Lee Hansen in his 1927 article in the *American Historical Review* called for the creation of archives and libraries of records of the immigrant experience. A decade later, this proposition was seconded by Louis Adamic, that zealous advocate of a pluralist America. But such proposals were not well received by the mainstream custodians of history; with few exceptions, archives, libraries, and historical societies regarded materials in other-than-English and of immigrant origin as of little, or no, historical value. In this respect, they shared the Melting Pot ideology of the historical profession itself. Prior to the 1960s, what systematic preservation of immigrant records took place was due to the initiatives of immigrant/ethnic historical societies, such as the American Jewish Historical Society, the Norwegian American Historical Association, the Polish Museum of America, etc. These organizations did invaluable work, although often limited by inadequate resources and lack of professional staff; but many immigrant groups did not have such institutions. In fact, many immigrants--and even more their children--were so marginalized by orthodox American history that they did not think they had a meaningful past; hence, they failed to value their records as historically significant (an attitude which we continue to encounter among ethnic Americans). As a consequence, a vast amount of documentation of the century of mass migrations (1830-1930) was permanently lost.[6]

In the 1960s—in response to the influences which were transforming American society's historical self concept—we became aware of the urgent need to save the surviving records of the great immigrations. In part, we were motivated by the awareness that the generations of immigrants were rapidly passing from the scene and their memories and their documents were being buried with them. This was literally true when entire ethnic neighborhoods were bulldozed in the "urban renewal" craze of the 1950s, churches, lodge halls, businesses, as well as homes were demolished, and often their records were buried in the debris. As we went about the task of searching out and collecting immigrant materials, however, we were pleasantly surprised to discover that large and rich collections of documents had by some miracle survived. The "miracle" was often in the person of some self-appointed lay custodian of the community's history (the unsung heroes of ethnic preservation). The commonplace, to which archivists, librarians, and historians had subscribed as a justification for their inaction, that immigrants were largely illiterate and inarticulate and therefore left no records to speak of, proved to be untrue.

As historians began more and more to aspire to do history not only from the "bottom up," but also from the "inside out," the demand for primary sources created by the immigrants themselves increased. Skeptical of "outsiders'" accounts of immigrant life by settlement workers, bureaucrats, and employers, historians wished to hear what the immigrants had to say in their own words. Oral histories, letters, memoirs, diaries, records of mutual aid societies, churches, labor groups, which gave access to their minds, hearts, and very souls, became the preferred sources for a new immigration history. As monographs on various immigrant groups multiplied, an awareness grew of the richness and complexity of the internal histories of these ethnic communities. This in turn generated yet more demands for sources reflecting the spectrum of political, religious, and social differences within the groups. Meanwhile, the application of cliometric techniques of analysis to the study of demography, mobility, and other aspects of immigrant life enhanced the value of individual-level data sources such as church registers and fraternal records. In short, a more sophisticated scholarship of immigration history generated the need for and in turn was stimulated by an expanding universe of documentation. Archives and libraries responded to this growing demand. State, city and county historical societies, university archives and special collections, as well as institutions such as the Center for Migration Studies and the Balch Institute, initiated more or less vigorous campaigns of building immigrant/ethnic collections.

Certainly we are immeasureably better off today than we were thirty years ago with respect to documentation of the immigrant experience. Hundreds of files of ethnic newspapers have been microfilmed, thousands of oral histories recorded, scores of archives of ethnic institutions preserved. What then, one might ask, is the problem? The problem is that we have thus far dealt with the proverbial tip of the iceberg.

Let me speak directly from the experience of the Immigration History Research Center, which has been in the business of collecting such records for a quarter of a century. Despite generous assistance from the National Endowment for the Humanities, the National Historical Publications and Records Commission, the Northwest Area Foundation, and—not least—the ethnic communities themselves, our resources have never been adequate to the magnitude of the task. It has been a continuing source of frustration that we have been able to respond to only a small fraction of the opportunities for collection development.

That in itself would not be troublesome if other institutions were willing and able to acquire the materials in question. However, that has usually not been the case. In addition, a large backlog of unprocessed collections limit their accessibility to researchers. Insufficient staff, resources, and space have been and continue to be a constant constraint. The IHRC is, I am certain, not unique in that respect. Part of the problem, which I hope this conference will address, is that of resources. How do we get the additional funding to do a more adequate job of documenting the immigrant experience?[7]

But there is more to it than that. We also need to address how we can utilize our resources more effectively: through the application of new technologies and management policies; through the development of more precise criteria for evaluating records; through the creation of inter-institutional consortia for information-sharing, exchanges, and division of labor. Although there is a good deal of ad hoc cooperation among institutions, we need to consider whether more formal arrangements would be advantageous. How can those of us engaged in collecting and preserving immigrant records work more effectively together to achieve our common ends? In this respect, I think it very important to include within the networks of consultation and mutual assistance not only academic institutions but also the ethnic historical societies and institutions, which probably still hold the greater part of this documentation. I also believe that it is very important for us to keep always in mind that these documents belong to the ethnic communities; if they come to our institutions as gifts, we thereby become trustees of the history and heritage of these groups.

Not surprisingly, given the trans-national character of the migrations, the challenge of documentation has an international dimension to it. Among the early historians of immigration, Theordore Blegen and George Stephenson were perhaps the first to search out "America" letters as a prime source for documenting the thoughts and feelings of the immigrants.[8] Other migration scholars in recent years have profitably exploited state and church archives in countries of emigration. In fact, today no study can claim to be comprehensive that has not been researched in both country of origin and destination. As migration studies have flourished in the countries of emigration, important, previously unknown bodies of records have surfaced. One thinks of the project directed by Wolfgang Helbich to collect "America" letters at the University of Bochum, or the Biella Project sponsored by the Sella Foundation, which turned up a great many letters, memoirs, and other documents of the emigrants; others could be mentioned.[9]

Clearly any project to inventory and facilitate access to sources on immigration to the United States must encompass materials in other countries. Since the documentation of the immigrant experience is international in nature, so must the strategies for collecting, preservation, and access be international in character. While several participants from

44

other countries are here to share their experiences with us, essentially the purpose of this conference is for us Americans to get our act together. The next stage of consultation should include a much broader representation of historians and archivists engaged in migration research in other countries.

While the references in my presentation might suggest a "Eurocentric" view, that is certainly not the conception underlying this conference. The planning committee's purpose was to take a global perspective, inclusive of all immigrants to the United States in the 19th and 20th centuries. That is clear from the composition of the participants. In the discussions of the planning committee, concern was particularly expressed about addressing the documentation of the newest immigrations from Central and South America, the Caribbean, the Near East, and Asia. While these post-1965 migrations may not yet have passed into the purview of immigration history, measures need to be taken now to gather and preserve their records so that the neglect of the past will not be repeated. We invite your advice on how this can best be done.

The second objective of this conference, the consideration of a documentary history of American immigration, is a logical outgrowth of the first. As the wealth of immigrant records in our libraries and archives increases, the question of access becomes more pressing. Beyond the use of such materials by researchers, are there ways in which we can make these extraordinary sources available to a larger public? Certainly, the immigrant letter, diary, photograph, minute book, sermon, would be eagerly used for curriculum materials, media presentations, journalistic writings, and sheer reading joyment by lay persons. However, the barriers of archival/library research—and often of language—deny access for such uses. There may be other ways to unlock such riches for the general culture (and we invite suggestions to that end), but one plausible answer is a multi-volume collection of selected and translated documents representing a range of immigrant groups as well as a variety of themes. We need your advice: How might such a documentary history be organized? administered? funded?

This conference has an ambitious scope. Presisely for that reason, we believe that it can make an important contribution, not just to the study of immigration history, but to a better understanding by Americans of the pluralistic character of their country and, hopefully, of other countries as well. That many of you have traveled many miles to be with us indicates that you share our sense of the significance of the enterprise in which we are engaged. I look forward to two days of lively, substantive, provocative discussions. I thank you for coming and for your contributions to our deliberations.

Notes

1. The members of the History Committee include Kathleen Neils Conzen, Roger Daniels, Jay P. Dolan, Victor R. Greene, F. Ross Holland, Jr., Louise Año Nuevo Kerr, Alan Kraut, Bara Levin, Dwight Pitcaithly, Moses Rischin, Rudolph J. Vecoli, and Virginia Yans-McLaughlin.

2. To date the series includes the following volumes: Gary R. Mormino and George E. Pozzetta, *The World of Ybor City: Italians and Their Latin Neighbors in Tampa, 1885-1985*; David M. Emmons, *The Butte Irish: Class and Ethnicity in an American Mining Town, 1875-1925*; David A. Gerber, *The Making of an American Pluralism: Buffalo, New York, 1825-60*; Frederick C. Luebke, *Germans in the New World: Essays in the History of Immigration*; and Rudolph J. Vecoli and Suzanne M. Sinke, eds., *A Century of European Migrations, 1830-1930*.

3. The papers from this conference have been published: Virginia Yans-McLaughlin, ed., *Immigration Reconsidered: History, Sociology, and Politics* (New York: Oxford University Press, 1990).

4. For an "official" history see Barbara Blumberg, *Celebrating the Immigrant: An Administrative History of the Statue of Liberty National Monument 1951-1982*, Cultural Resource Management Study No. 10, North Atlantic Regional Office, National Park Service, U.S. Department of the Interior (1985); but also John Bodnar, "Symbols and Servants: Immigrant America and the Limits of Public History," *Journal of American History* 73 (1986), 137-151.

5. I further explore the reasons for the shift in historical paradigms in these articles: "Louis Adamic and the American Search for Roots," *Ethnic Studies* (Monash University, Australia) 2 (1978), 29-35; "Return to the Melting Pot: Ethnicity in the United States in the Eighties," *Journal of American Ethnic History* 5 (1985), 7-20; "From *The Uprooted* to *The Transplanted*: The Writing of American Immigration History, 1951-1989," in Valeria Gennaro Lerda, ed., *From "Melting Pot" to Multiculturalism: The Evolution of Ethnic Relations in the United States and Canada* (Rome: Bulzoni Editore, 1990), 25-53.

6. Marcus Lee Hansen, "The History of American Immigration as a Field of Research," *American Historical Review* 32 (1927), 500-518; Louis Adamic, *From Many Lands* (New York, 1940), 347-49; Rudolph J. Vecoli, "Ethnicity: A Neglected Dimension of American History," in Herbert J. Bass, ed., *The State of American History* (Chicago: Quadrangle, 1970), 70-88.

7. For our experience with the Immigration History Research Center, see Rudolph J. Vecoli, "The Immigration Studies Collection of the University of Minnesota," *American Archivist* 32 (1969), 139-45; idem., "Diamonds in Your Own Backyard": Developing Documentation on European Immigrants in North America," *Ethnic Forum* 1 (1981), 2-16; Suzanna Moody and Joel Wurl, eds. and comps., *The Immigration History Research Center: A Guide to Collections* (Westport, CT: Greenwood Press, 1991).

8. Theodore Blegen, ed., *Land of Their Choice: The Immigrants Write Home* (Minneapolis: University of Minnesota Press, 1955); George Stephenson, *The Religious Aspects of Swedish Immigration: A Study of Immigrant Churches* (Minneapolis: University of Minnesota Press, 1932).

9. Writings by non-Americans on the immigration history of the United States are reported in Lewis Hanke, ed., *Guide to the Study of United States History Outside the U.S., 1945-1980,* 5 vols. (White Plains, NY: Kraus International Publications, 1985); for examples of migration scholarship based on sources abroad, see Harald Runblom and Hans Norman, eds., *From Sweden to America: A History of Emigration* (Minneapolis: University of Minnesota Press, 1976); Valerio Castronovo, ed., *Biellesi nel Mondo,* 2 vols. (Milan: Edizioni Electra, 1986-1988). Among the documents turned up by the latter project are the letters published in Samuel L. Baily and Franco Ramella, eds., *One Family, Two Worlds: An Italian Family's Correspondence Across the Atlantic, 1901-1922* (New Brunswick: Rutgers University Press, 1988).

Archivists and Immigrants, Embarking for New Destinations Together

John J. Grabowski

It is impossible to forego the temptation to draw an analogy between the work of archivists who attempt to develop new collections and the process of migration and immigration. Both involve a journey with a specific goal in mind—for the archivist it is the accumulation of data relating to a subject such as immigration, for the immigrant it is usually economic betterment. Both the immigrant and the archivist are drawn or driven to their goals for a variety of reasons.

For the archivist interested in immigration history the impetus may be conscience, personal conviction, or an anxious research community—the attraction may be the hope of new users and new support. Like the immigrant or migrant the archivist learns much along the way: the route may be rougher than imagined, it may involve diversions not at all expected, and the resources planned for the journey may prove far too lean. Most importantly, on reaching the destination, the archivist, like the immigrant or migrant, often finds it not the end point it was imagined to be. Nothing is settled, nothing fully consummated. The collections accumulated on the journey are good, but not good enough; there is no sense of cohesion or community at that same destination; and most critically, there is a sense of goals unfulfilled and opportunities yet to be pursued.

This analogy does somewhat reflect the current status of those of us involved in the accumulation and preservation of immigrant-related archival resources. We have reached a point where we have arrived somewhere in terms of the collections we have acquired, and where we have built a community of practitioners—the size of which remains uncertain. But most importantly, in the time since we embarked on this journey, the nature of our profession, and the nature of research in the fields of immigration and ethnicity, has shifted and evolved. Within this changing milieu archivists must now reexamine their original intentions and, given a new set of professional requirements, simultaneously evaluate their present status, and plan for a new destination.

To do so, archivists must recall where they started. Thirty years ago, the field of ethnic manuscript collecting within academic or mainline historical institutions simply did not exist. Only the ethnic groups themselves, through agencies such as the Polish American Museum, the American Jewish Archives, colleges such as St. Olaf, and a myriad of small reading rooms and "national" libraries, preserved some part of the primary record of the immigrant experience in America.[1]

At that time, in the early 1960s, there arose within the academic community a burgeoning interest in social history and with it an investigative interest in the history of immigration and the nature of ethnicity in America. That phenomenon, more than anything else, spurred the development of ethnic collections within mainline archival institutions as some custodians of the American primary record sought to meet new research needs.[2] In an ironic turn of fate many of those who came to build the new collections were the students of the new social historians--students who, in a shrinking academic job market, found positions as archivists and curators and therein put to very practical use the lessons they had absorbed from their mentors. That many of these new curators and archivists shared an immigrant ancestry dating from the post-1880 period, is both an interesting fact and a critical piece of evidence that explains the passion with which they pursued both cause and collection. Some thirty years later, however, professionalism has been expected to subsume passion.[3]

By the early 1980s these "ethnic archivists" had helped create the national and large regional collections at the Immigration History Research Center at the University of Minnesota and the Balch Institute for Ethnic Studies in Philadelphia. Others initiated smaller geographically-focused efforts in ethnic-based collecting at institutions such as Kent State University, the University of Pittsburgh, the Chicago Historical Society, the Western Reserve Historical Society in Cleveland, the State Historical Society of Wisconsin, and the Minnesota Historical Society. Even within the immigrant communities themselves, the awakening of interest in ethnicity fostered new archival programs. Twenty-five percent of the institutions listed in Lubomyr Wynar's 1980 guide to Slavic ethnic libraries and archives listed a post-1960 founding date.[4] Where there had once been a vacuum, there stood, by the mid-1980s, scores of repositories with an expressed interest in the subject. It is hard to measure this growth. Philip Hamer's 1961 *Guide to Manuscripts and Archives in the United States* listed eight repositories having collections relevant to immigration. Seventeen years later, the *NHPRC Directory of Archives and Manuscript Repositories in the United States* listed 152 institutions holding material relating to immigration and ethnicity although for 92 of these institutions the reported material related to the Germans. Newer immigrant groups fell into the collecting scope of only a small number of institutions reporting in that guide.[5]

The exact scale of what occurred since 1960 has yet to be determined, for much more may be in progress at institutions that, for one reason or another, do not report to national guides. This may be particularly true for regionally- centered repositories that may have included immigration as part of their social history collecting menu in the years since the 1960s but have not seen it as a predominant part of their mission. How many of the city, state or county repositories listed in the NHPRC guide, for instance, cite geography rather than a specific subject area, such as immigration, as the focus of their collections but yet may have acquired relevant immigrant materials? It is possible that many such repositories may have been enticed into collecting immigrant records, particularly if their staff was exposed to the papers on ethnic and social history collecting have been part and parcel of archival meetings on state, regional and national levels since the early 1970s.[6]

Whatever their intentions, the degree of success achieved by these collecting programs is still a matter of conjecture. We know that the collections of agencies such as the Immigration History Research Center and the Balch have grown enormously. But what of the overall picture? What materials have the other agencies acquired? If one examines the numbers of collections reported to the National Union Catalog of Manuscript Collections under the heading "immigration and emigration," there is a sense of growth. Thirty-one listings are given under this heading in the 1959-1962 NUCMC index, 109 in the 1967-69 index, and 121 in the 1980-1984 index.[7]

Whether these figures represent new materials or the retroactive reporting of older collections is an open question. As the reports to NUCMC are voluntary we see only a part of the picture when reviewing these volumes. Whatever portion of the whole they represent, one can assume that the reporting of these figures is, at least, evidence of interest in the field, as in one instance they might signal new collecting efforts, and in the other an awareness that older holdings of immigrant-related collections are important enough to be reported. Of course, the figures in NUCMC could simply reflect the increasing professionalism and sophistication in the archival community during this period, where more and more agencies recognized the need to list their holdings in a nationally-accessible format.

If perusing the pages of NUCMC presents some frustrations to the researcher looking for the growth of immigrant-related collections, the future may prove more troublesome as on-line reporting of collections to utilities such as RLIN and OCLC displaces traditional hard copy. Whatever their potential, these computerized databases may obscure the collections held by agencies too poor to go on-line but which may have reported on paper to NUCMC.[8]

It will be interesting, in this same vein, in several years, to review the results of the U.S. Newspaper Repository Project sponsored by NEH. What percentage of the titles reported by all manner of repositories will be immigrant-related? In this case though, the state-based NEH programs which survey and report the holdings of non-on-line libraries may allow for a more complete analysis of ethnic newspaper holdings. Centralized control and coordination are the key to comprehensiveness in this project. This type of survey and report format might serve as a model for analyzing ethnic archival holdings.

Whatever the explanation for the NUCMC figures, or the final total of titles from the NEH database, they will reflect only a miniscule portion of the immigrant-related material available to archivists. The broad scattering and potential value of such material has caused it to be characterized by Rudolph Vecoli as "diamonds" in one's own backyard.[9] The term backyard is most appropriate, since the effects and history of immigration and ethnicity are largely a local phenomenon in the United States. We have yet to count, for instance, the number of "Little Italies" in America. Certainly they are to be found in larger cities such as New York, Chicago, Cleveland and Youngstown. But they can also be found in small towns like Barre, Vermont, and Casper, Wyoming. Change the group from Italian, to Polish or Hungarian, and the number of cities, towns and collecting possibilities multiplies geometrically.

Surveys of fraternal records conducted by the Immigration History Research Center, and of immigrant materials in the anthracite region of Pennsylvania conducted by the Balch Institute, have graphically indicated the substantial amounts of papers and records which could be considered for archival preservation.[10] The city of Cleveland, Ohio, has at this time 58 ethnic and racial groups that maintain some sort of organizational activity and, therefore, produce records.[11] The sheer number of contemporary ethnic organizations and contemporary newspaper publications listed in the several guides compiled by Lubomyr Wynar makes one wonder just how enormous a body of material has been and is being produced.[12] We have, indeed, crossed an ocean in getting to this point and we are only beginning to fathom its depth.

If we have, in the last thirty years, come to realize that there are a multitude of sources for immigrant-related materials, we have also begun to realize how diverse they are and, in many cases, how different from what we may have expected. Curators in immigrant archives moved off on a traditionally directed journey looking for letters, diaries and other standard personal papers, as well as the correspondence, minutes and ledgers of ethnic organizations. In general, the initial efforts were directed toward seeking such traditional materials within a broad spectrum of individuals and organizations. Eventually, the process of collecting led to a clearer understanding of the organizations and types of material that had the greatest value.

Rudolph Vecoli has pointed out the importance of the records of the three cornerstones of many ethnic communities: the church, the fraternal organization, and the newspaper.[13] Within these areas archivists began to find non-traditional documents of value—including insurance applications for fraternals, the ubiquitous anniversary pamphlets issued by a variety of community organizations, and the annuals or kalandari published by fraternals and the ethnic newspapers themselves. Indeed, in instances such as the kalandari and the newspapers, the archivists found themselves dealing with printed rather than manuscript sources. While finding new materials of value, archivists also found fewer traditional documents—diaries and detailed personal correspondence—than expected.[14]

As collecting progressed in the 1960s and 1970s and archivists became aware of the nature of American ethnic records, they also discovered ancillary sources that, perhaps, also deserved their attention. In particular, the mainline agencies that dealt with immigrants, such as the International Institutes, settlement houses, and local government immigrant bureaus, along with those who employed immigrants—factories, railroads, and a variety of businesses—all produced records that presented additional collecting challenges. Then, as researchers began to look at American immigration as not merely an end-point phenomenon but one with equally important beginnings, the value of materials in Europe became obvious. Fortunately, surveys like the ones conducted by the University of Michigan in the early 1970s found many such materials already accessible in foreign archives. But then the question arose as to how much of this material needed to be made intellectually available to an American audience through either guides or copies.[15]

While the scope of ethnic sources assumed ever larger proportions, so did collection size. Expecting a small volume of diaries and letters, archivists instead often discovered basements full of the records of fraternal insurance organizations. The files of major multi-state fraternals like the Polish National Alliance and the Sons of Italy, as well as the records of agencies such as the International Institutes, were measured not in dozens of linear feet, but in hundreds. The acquisition of one such collection could overwhelm an archival agency, taxing not only space, but the agency's ability to administer name-sensitive records such as applications and case files.

The further archivists progressed toward their destination, the more complex became the patterns of their journey. The problems presented by the variety and size of the sources being sought were compounded by the fragility of the materials since the focus of many collecting efforts—the coming of the peoples of the great post-1880s immigration—was, unfortunately, an event contemporaneous with the wood pulp paper era. Not only the newspapers, but the books, anniversary pamphlets, and even the writing paper of the people whose experiences they sought to preserve were often composed of highly acidic paper. Within the immigrant communities, publishers operating on marginal budgets used the cheapest material available to produce affordable items for a readership for which the purchase of any item beyond food and shelter was an issue of the most careful consideration. It is, as yet, unproven, but suspected that the fugitive nature of the documents relating to immigrants and ethnicity in this period far exceeds that of those which relate to contemporary groups more firmly associated with the American mainstream.[16]

This problem, at least in the area of newspaper preservation, generated early and concerted action by several repositories, including the Immigration History Research Center and the Center for Research Libraries, which, with the aid of National Endowment for the Humanities funds and funds from the ethnic communities themselves, began microfilming programs directed toward the Polish, Ukrainian and other ethnic presses. More promises to be done in this area as the NEH continues to fund its Newspaper Repositories survey, with the preservation of all parts of the American press as an ultimate goal.[17] The fate, however, of embrittled ethnic books, pamphlets and ephemera remains unresolved. One can only hope that the current concern with "slow fires" and the embrittled book will extend to these lesser known items, the importance of which had not been realized until the initial phase of ethnic archival accumulation.[18]

The issues discussed to this point fall into the category of personal revelations that the immigrant archivists have accumulated during their journey. They alone provide cause to reflect on the reason for, and purpose of, that journey. However, their unsettling tendencies are compounded by changes both in the uses of immigrant-related resources and in the philosophy of the archival profession. Like many immigrants, archivists have left one shore for another only to find that the rules of conduct have changed.

The initial efforts at collecting constituted an attempt to permit a previously unheard and inarticulate part of America to speak. Given this archivists were pleased to collect whatever narrative records they could, only to learn from some researchers and through self-revelation that they, perhaps, were documenting a literate elite within the immigrant communities. The true story of the immigrants was, some historians felt, to be discovered through cliometrics. Vast statistics, already available in a variety of governmental and bureaucratic records, were the key to immigration history. Other researchers challenged the cold aloofness of statistics as well as the "elite" nature of standard narrative sources and suggested oral interview as the only means of allowing the inarticulate to speak. As attractive as oral history appeared, it represented both a conceptual and fiscal challenge not easily met by many institutions. Combinations of these techniques were also suggested. Archivists thus found themselves pulled in a variety of directions as what had begun as a simple collecting program was evolving into a complex and increasingly expensive set of issues centering around the veracity and viability of sources.[19]

By the mid-1980s a number of archivists collecting in a variety of social history fields began to sit down and take stock of what they had accomplished. For many, the work had produced enormous results. Stacks were filled with collections. For the most part, however, the collections were unprocessed, largely unavailable and, when closely examined, provided only a scattered overview of the subjects they purported to document. Ethnic collections in a geographically-centered repository, for instance, might relate to only several of the many ethnic groups that resided in the region. Even if a single group was represented by a number of collections, these did not provide a seamless web of information. Fraternal groups might be well represented, while the records of choral societies, political organizations and women's clubs were not within the holdings. Researchers looking for information on Polish women at the Western Reserve Historical Society will find that the agency has the records of the main two local male fraternals on microfilm, but not those of any local women's groups. It does, however, hold the records of local Czech women's groups. Such lapses in coverage within groups or within subject areas overarching numbers of immigrant groups were a problem that was recognized in many of the collections by the mid-1980s.[20]

While the solution to such problems would seem to be more collecting designed to fill such gaps, the answer was not quite that simple. By the time archivists realized such gaps existed they also knew that enormous resources would have to be dedicated to process what had already been collected. Other resources would have to be devoted to the construction of buildings and the employment of technologies to preserve those collections. By the mid-1980s the idealistic new archivists of the 1960s, who perceived few limits and who felt a missionary zeal in the cause of preserving everyone's history, had come up against the wall of dollars-and-cents reality. There was too much for any one person or agency to do and too little money to go around.

The idealists of the sixties also confronted a changing archival profession. Whereas collection building was a common topic of archival literature in the 1960s and 1970s, management, planning, and professionalism became the watchwords of the 1980s. American archival practice, unlike its European counterpart, grew out of the history graduate schools of American beginning in the 1930s. It was, therefore, much more sympathetic to historical research needs than it would, perhaps, have been had it had the same administrative/functional bent characteristic of its European counterpart.

There has been, however, a shift away from Clio as an American archival muse in the past ten years. It has occurred when archivists—largely those serving institutional needs in business or government—became less active as the custodians of the organizational memory and more involved in the contemporary information management needs of their employers. To compete successfully within the structure of 1980s corporate America they had to learn to manage, cooperate and produce. The issues confronting them became a part of the 1980s archival agenda and, in turn, affected their colleagues active in the areas of manuscripts and special collections.

This more academic cadre of the profession also had its own new challenges to meet as curators realized that the preservation of the entire record of the recent past might be an impossibility in a world of limited resources. Their shift in philosophy toward an emphasis on appraisal, reappraisal, management, cooperation, and collection control shares much with the outlook of their institutional colleagues. It is hard to translate this yet ongoing change into terms meaningful for this essay. It might be sufficient to say that now, in archives, historical idealism and zeal must be subordinated to fiscal reality, and that archivists and curators must learn to adhere to the dictates of a society that views the management of information, whether for institutional purposes or research, as part of a rationally organized system that has a bottom line of efficiency, profit or broadly perceived public purpose.

For those who entered upon the journey as immigrant archivists, changes in the profession, such as certification, training in management, and the creation of documentation strategies, might appear to be draconian abrogations of academic and archival freedom. That, however, would be a substantial misjudgment, for while certain changes may present problems, others, which attempt to cope with the limited resources allocated to the archival profession, may allow archivists to cope with some of the problems that they, as immigrant archivists, discovered in their journey to this point. In particular, the creation of firm documentation strategies and collection policies, and the employment of collection analysis and user surveys can only help archivists direct their resources to the most important of the myriad of sources they might collect. At the same time, the tool of management, particularly when viewed as cooperative planning among scholars, archivists and institutions in the solution of a specific problem—in this case the collection and preservation of immigrant-related resources—will permit archivists to do a better job by allocating responsibilities and sharing burdens.

Archivists documenting the American immigrant experience have arrived at their first destination. They need now to come together, share the stories of the journey, cooperatively discover the lay of the land and, using both the concern and commitment they packed with them thirty years ago, and the techniques they will acquire in this new 1990s archival world, embark for a new destination that will provide for a greater fulfillment of their hope of preserving this nation's immigrant heritage.

Notes

1.   Rudolph J. Vecoli, "The Immigration Studies Collection of the University of Minnesota," *The American Archivist* 32 (April 1969), 139-145. This article discusses the beginning of the Minnesota program and details some of the immigrant-supported collections in existence in the early 1960s.

2.   A history research project relating to the Minnesota Iron Ranges led to the establishment of the Immigration History Research Center. Vecoli, "The Immigration Studies Collection," 142-143. See also Richard J. Juliani, "The Use of Archives in the Study of Immigration and Ethnicity," *The American Archivist* 39 (October 1976), 469-478, for the linkage between interest in the "new" history and the growth of immigrant/ethnic collections. Gerald Ham, "The Archival Edge," *The American Archivist* 38 (January 1975), 5-13, discusses the archivist's role in providing for a fuller documentation of the American experience.

3.   No one has yet fully compiled and analyzed the names and ethnic backgrounds of individuals active in creating immigrant/ethnic archives. The names seem overwhelmingly to derive from origins among the "new" or post-1880 immigration. Among those who have been or are active are Rudolph Vecoli, Frank Zabrosky, Mary Cygan, Mark Stolarik, Nicholas Montalto, John Bodnar, and Frank Renkiewicz.

4.   Lubomyr R. Wynar, *Slavic Ethnic Libraries, Museums and Archives in the United States: A Guide and Directory* (Chicago: American Library Association, 1980). See also Wynar and Lois Buttlar, *Guide to Ethnic Museums, Libraries, and Archives in the United States* (Kent, OH: Program for the Study of Ethnic Publications, School of Library Science, Kent State University, 1978) for a reflection of this expansion of collecting and heritage awareness among a larger number of ethnic groups.

5.   This analysis is based on a count of agencies reporting holdings pertinent to the index category of "immigration and emigration" and national subdivision listed thereunder. Holdings linked to index entries for specific ethnic groups were not counted. National

Historical Publications and Records Commission, *Directory of Archives and Manuscript Repositories in the United States* (New York: Oryx Press, 1988).

6. See annual meeting programs for the Society of American Archivists and biannual programs for smaller organizations such as the Midwest Archives Conference and the Society of Ohio Archivists dating from the 1970s. At least one session on minority collecting can usually be found each year within the programs sponsored by these organizations.

7. Library of Congress Catalogs, *National Union Catalog of Manuscript Collections* (Washington: Indexes for years noted in text).

8. The current trend for reporting manuscript materials on a national basis is through use of the MARC-AMC manuscripts format on one of the two major national utilities, OCLC or RLIN. The current cost (Western Reserve Historical Society figures) of linkage to the national OCLC cataloging utility is $400 per month exclusive of equipment and search charges.

9. Rudolph J. Vecoli, "Diamonds in Your Own Backyard: Developing Documentation on European Immigrants to North America," *Ethnic Forum* 1 (September 1981), 2-16.

10. For a discussion of surveys and their utility as a collection planning tool see R. Joseph Anderson, "Managing Change and Chance: Collecting Policies in Social History Archives," *The American Archivist* 48 (Summer 1985), 296-303, and Nicholas J. Montalto, "The Challenge of Preservation in a Pluralistic Society: A Report of the Immigration History Research Center, University of Minnesota," *The American Archivist* 41 (October 1978), 399-404.

11. Nationalities Services Center, *Cleveland Ethnic Directory* (Cleveland: by the Center, 1990).

12. Lubomyr R. Wynar and Anna T. Wynar, *Encyclopedic Directory of Ethnic Newspapers and Periodicals in the United States* (Littleton, Colorado: Libraries Unlimited, 1976).

13. Vecoli, "Diamonds in Your Own Backyard," 6-12.

14. Juliani, "The Use of Archives," points out the difficulties in locating and preserving personal documents such as letters. Juliani believes that such materials might be located, albeit with extraordinary effort and new collecting techniques. However, in reviewing lists of holdings of the Immigration History Research Center, the Western Reserve Historical Society, and the accessions reported in the newsletter *New Dimensions* of the Balch Institute, collections of correspondence and diaries of "minor" figures seem to form only a small portion of the materials accumulated to date.

15. Robert M. Warner and Francis X. Blouin, Jr., "Documenting the Great Migration and a Century of Ethnicity in America," *The American Archivist* 39 (July 1976), 319-328. This article discusses the European archival surveys conducted by the University of Michigan.

16. Only impressionistic evidence gathered by the author during twenty years of work in the field can be cited as support for this statement at present. This is based on handling collections of ethnic publications (novels, guidebooks, etc.) issued in the United States since the 1880s. Many were printed by ethnic newspaper publishers who simply used highly acidic newspaper stock for the pages of the books they issued. See, for example, the various hardbound books issued in Polish by the Paryski Publishing Company of Toledo, Ohio.

17. Montalto, "The Challenge of Preservation," discusses the newspaper projects undertaken at the Immigration History Research Center.

18. Some publications, such as the anniversary programs issued by numerous immigrant organizations, seem, at first glance, to have little lasting value. However, they often contain histories of the organization, membership lists, and statements of purpose that cannot be found elsewhere in the historical record. Often printed on highly-acidic stock (particularly if issued by a smaller or relatively new organization) these can be critical for many aspects of scholarly inquiry. See John J. Grabowski, "Ethnic Ephemera and Newsprint: A Case for Better Bibliographic Control," *Ethnic Forum* 2 (Fall 1982).

19. Juliani, "The Use of Archives," discusses the potential value of oral history in documenting the immigrant experience. The time, care, and expense involved in creating historically viable oral interviews is addressed in Willa K. Baum, *Oral History for the Local Historical Society* (Nashville: American Association for State and Local History, 1971). This basic guide to "doing" oral history clearly points out the investments that need to be made in preparation time and in transcription and reference presentation.

20. Grigg, "A World of Repositories, a World of Records: Redefining the Scope of a National Subject Collection," *The American Archivist* 48 (Summer 1985), 286-295 analyzes the effectiveness/comprehensiveness of early efforts at immigrant collection development. Anderson, "Managing Change and Chance," discusses the possible strategies to be employed for comprehensive collection development.

The Archival Golden Door: Thoughts on Improving the State of Historical Documentation on the Immigrant Experience

Joel Wurl

In preparing this paper, I racked my brain to come up with a simple metaphor to embody the current state of documentation on the American immigrant experience—something in the fine tradition of "uprooting," "transplanting," melting pots, and mosaics. In an earlier article on this subject, I likened the universe of immigration-related repositories to an untended garden in which the various individual plants, although sharing common ground, were sprouting and maturing independently and haphazardly.[1] But for this presentation I wanted something else, with stronger elements of destiny, movement, and barriers to progress.

Then it happened. Rudy returned from the Ellis Island Museum opening ceremonies with a copy of the new Ellis Island coloring book, which on page 23 contains the immigration maze. "Guide the new immigrant through processing," it implores. I knew I had my comparative image; the caption on another such maze could read "Help the historian find her way to the right documentation," or "Help the archivists ensure adequate and accessible documentation of American immigration." While this minor revelation did not inspire a new one- or two-word catch phrase (I did toy with "the re-routed"), it gave me a framework for organizing my observations.

The documentation maze facing the average researcher is a tangled mess. Here is a rough hypothetical synopsis of what might confront a doctoral student preparing a dissertation on the Hungarian community of Toledo, Ohio. Will the student find useful primary sources? Indeed he will, if he is diligent and lucky. The mere fact that there proves to be a fair number of possibilities to explore makes this a happier scenario than that witnessed by researchers of many other ethnic topics.

But the student's satisfaction in beginning to uncover material is soon dampened by the realization of how decentralized, uncoordinated, and idiosyncratic the accumulation of these sources has been. He probably discovers early on that the Toledo Public library has made a special effort to document the city's so-called Birmingham neighborhood, in part through an extensive videotaped oral history project. But he also notes considerable gaps in that repository's holdings. Some of these gaps, he finds, are filled

61

by the Center for Archival Collections at nearby Bowling Green State University, the Ohio regional history and local government records network site for the Toledo area. In establishing connections between Toledo's Hungarians and their fellow countrymen and women in Detroit and Cleveland, he is introduced to relevant material in the Burton Historical Collection at the Detroit Public Library and in the Western Reserve Historical Society. Then he falls upon citations to a more distant institution affiliated with the University of Minnesota, which purports to be one of the leading repositories of primary documentation on Hungarians in the United States and which indeed does have useful information on his topic.

Back in Toledo, he learns, there are some lesser explored caches. There's the city's International Institute, which supposedly is still holding a large volume of its inactive records, and there's the University of Toledo Library, which endeavors to build an extensive collection of imprints from the area's ethnic publishers. Of course, a number of Toledo's Hungarians would have been involved in fraternal activity. Lo and behold, the largest Hungarian fraternal, the William Penn Association, is currently in the process of establishing a new facility for its own archives and for material on Hungarian Americans more generally. As the student investigates questions of labor, religion, or inter-ethnic group relations, a myriad of other potential resources and repositories is revealed—and he hasn't even crossed the Atlantic yet.

The scattered whereabouts of the material is by no means the only problem our student encounters. Each place he visits presents a unique adventure in identifying and obtaining access to the right documentation; impoverished archives and libraries are forced to improvise. The documents or newspapers he is handed are quite likely in disarray or disrepair, and the descriptive aids, if any exist other than a staff person's good memory, probably do not furnish the kind of detail and depth he had hoped for. And how is it that he came to learn of these repositories in the first place? If he found the most useful recent bibliographic product on Hungarian Americans—Steven and Agnes Vardy's lengthy article in the journal *Hungarian Studies*—it was almost certainly the result of a suggestion from a knowledgeable mentor or archivist and not of consulting any standard reference tools.[2] At the end of his project, would he assess the documentation he unearthed to be adequate for constructing the full story of Toledo's Hungarians? Even with the relatively large amount of material he could consult, I would expect him to point out large voids in the overall record.

Common Needs

I expect many of you can offer your own better accounts of weaving through the archival research maze. My aim in calling attention to these experiences and recollections is to set us on the starting block of a related but perhaps even more perplexing labyrinth. The remainder of my remarks will deal with the matter of advancing the current state of documentation on American immigration. My role, like that of the rest of the speakers, is to lay issues on the table for further dissection by the rest of you; and like those who have already spoken, I will certainly be serving up more questions than answers. But since our conference planning committee has continually stressed the desire to emerge from this gathering with some concrete recommendations for further action, I decided to try to nudge our discussions in that direction by making a handful of suggestions, which I've reserved for the end of my presentation.

The key element in any maze is the reward at the end. If we intend to embark from this conference upon a pathway leading to a better archival order, we should probably spend some time considering what this new order might actually look like. When I first set out to prepare this talk, I had it in mind to paint an elaborate picture of the ideal world for immigration source material and the people who use it and administer it. The futility of that struck home pretty quickly. However, I did conclude that there was some value in *attempting* to visualize what lies on the other side of the archival golden door.

All of us would recognize, and I think agree upon, several of the features that would comprise a more ideal situation for immigration documentation. Among these are the following: 1) sufficient staffing for every archives or library pertaining to immigration, including at least one individual with professional training or experience in archival work; 2) ample storage space for existing and future source material, with environmental control capability for preservation purposes; 3) basic research facilities and equipment at each site where documentation is housed; 4) convenient and more detailed descriptions of sources, including repository-level finding aids, multi-institutional guides, and/or automated networking; 5) a keen awareness on the part of private citizens and organizations regarding the value of ethnic documentation and the need to preserve and make it available. These are just some of the general categories; each of us has our own, more specific wish list.

One of the sadder realities we must confront is that this short list of aspirations represent the most fundamental types of requirements for servicing the documentary heritage of American immigration. We should not have to view them as utopian; they should already be in place, and we should not be needing a conference to help us identify the means to achieve them. But to a large extent, such is our condition, and it is not peculiar to the field of immigration history.

The characteristics I've outlined all have at least one thing in common: their realization would require a considerable infusion of money. As crucial as this fact is—and I will be returning to it—I believe there are several other ingredients that comprise an optimistic vision of immigrant documentation, ingredients not linked so tightly to monetary concerns.

Consider, for instance, the issue of collection building. The ideal state of affairs would encompass not only sufficient resources for locating, transferring, and accommodating new material, it would entail calculated decision making based on obtainable answers to various questions: What current research trends exist that require the availability of new primary source material? What are the collecting or accessioning missions of the various repositories related in some way to the subject or ethnic group at issue? What gaps are present in our knowledge of the subject or group? What makes up the universe of potential documentation from which new material can be solicited? What relevant source material *is* actually available in archives or libraries?

In an ideal view of things, acquisition work would be undertaken primarily in a proactive fashion, relying less upon serendipity. Repositories would be responsive to the needs of academic researchers and other user groups, but they would also serve to prod research along new paths by developing new acquisition initiatives. In short, collecting and accessioning practices would be implemented from a much broader perspective than that which is reflected in the traditional approach of determining simply if a given source fits with one's acquisition "policy."[3]

Other functions pertaining to the administration of primary source material would likewise be brought out of the separate procedural vacuums that have evolved in every institution. Cataloging and other descriptive methods would be characterized more by inter-institutional standardization than by unique internal access systems. The needs and interests of various researchers—not only academic—would play a more prominent role in the production of descriptive tools. Information on the availability of new material, either through acquisition or processing, would be communicated routinely among archivists and to researchers. Every repository would have a reliable source to turn to for technical guidance on processing and preserving ethnic documentation. Archivists and librarians would be well aware of their institutions' overlapping preservation needs and would regularly create ways to pool resources and expertise. Again, we could go on much further.

64

Common Problems

In attempting to visualize a better future, we should avoid any pretenses toward precision or comprehensiveness. I also believe we have to keep our ideals connected to practical reality, focusing only on what is actually feasible, at least in the foreseeable future. The several desired conditions I relayed above reside, I feel, within the realm of the do-able. but they are only do-able if a number of significant barriers are overcome. Like any ticklish maze, this one is lousy with road blocks.

The following summary of these road blocks is likely to lead us quickly into a mood of despair, so before providing that, I want to emphasize a more uplifting point. This conference has by no means been born of failure. Since the advent of the new social history movement and the reawakening of ethnic consciousness in the 1960s, a truly extraordinary amount of documentation has been preserved and made available in archives and libraries throughout the country, an observation shared earlier by both John and Rudy. The avalanche of secondary research on immigration and ethnicity over the past 25 years has benefited from *and* helped drive forward this activity. Virtually everyone in this room can take pride in having contributed in some way to this process. Clearly, a good deal of what has been done to document the immigrant experience up to now has worked; our task might prove to be less one of developing new strategies or methods than of isolating and employing the most successful approaches from the past and present. But although we can look to such accomplishments with satisfaction, we need to be mindful even more of how far we still need to go. Contentment with the status quo would constitute perhaps our most severe obstacle to progress.

Presuming that we *do* recognize the need, or at least the opportunity, for improving the current plight of documentation, it is impossible to talk about hurdles without putting funding at the top of the list. One colleague recently remarked, "There is no problem with respect to ethnic archives that cannot be resolved with a little bit of goodwill and a lot of money." Perhaps this should be revised to read, "there is no problem that *can* be resolved *without* a little bit of goodwill and a lot of money."

This conference must, as Rudy has said, consider the matter of resources and fund raising very carefully; for there are few, if any, projects we can launch without either the addition of new funds or the redeployment of existing resources. This is going to be an overwhelming challenge. Many archival institutions cannot make ends meet as it is, and beating the seemingly barren bushes for external support requires time and skills that many of us do not have. But as ominous as this problem is, we cannot allow it to paralyze us. As I indicated above, I believe that some of the tasks confronting us might actually depend more upon goodwill than money, and I am optimistic that solutions to some of our funding needs can be found. (Let me remind you that this opinion comes from someone who has just worked for a year at NEH.)

In contrast to the problem of limited resources, the scope of archives, libraries, museums, historical societies, and other repositories whose missions encompass the immigrant experience presents an obstacle because of its almost unbounded dimensions. In part, we are victims today of some of the success we have witnessed in accumulating documentation over the past thirty years. In the 1978 *Guide to Ethnic Museums, Libraries, and Archives in the United States*, Lubomyr Wynar and Lois Buttlar listed over 800 institutions within the ethnic communities themselves that were then involved in preserving primary research material.[4] How many more could be added from the past 12 years? To these, of course, must also be added the multiethnic research institutions, such as the Balch, CMS, and the IHRC as well as a countless number of state, regional, and local history programs at universities and public or private libraries. Repositories dealing with urban history, labor history, women's history, social welfare, religion, and other themes also carry immigration-related holdings. Government records, from the National Archives on down to the voluminous files of county courthouses must be factored in as do, of course, pertinent archives and research centers in the various countries of emigration. Then, too, it would seem appropriate to heed Victor Greene's recent advice to acquaint ourselves better with the existence of substantive collections amassed and administered by private individuals.[5]

How can this universe be defined or understood, let alone shaped in any systematic way? Imagine the time we had on the planning committee choosing 45 people to reflect this universe; we could not even hope to succeed in having one representative from each solar system. The effort to improve documentation of the immigrant experience will necessitate a more complete understanding of not only "who has what," but, since we are also considering preservation and access issues, "what they are doing with what they have." There is not now any centralized accumulation of such information, and producing one could be a massive undertaking.

The range of different types of primary source material within these repositories and in private hands appears also to be limitless. John has reminded us of Rudy's exhortations to archivists in the 1960s and 70s centering on the records of fraternals, churches, and the products of the immigrant press. But he and others recognized the importance of additional forms of documentation. Memoirs, "America letters," government reports, settlement house records, social case work files, photographs, census manuscripts, passenger lists, literary works, scrapbooks, and much, much more—all of these have become more abundantly available in archives throughout the country and have figured prominently in research projects.

Other, less "traditional" kinds of records must also be taken into account in any general assessment of documentation: oral histories, sound recordings and sheet music, films, works of art, radio broadcasts and scripts, and computerized sociological data files, to name just a few. Some of these sources are being preserved, but we have no clear idea of how thoroughly. My suspicion is that there are numerous kinds of records that archivists and researchers have barely tapped, if at all. The files of immigrant banks and other commercial enterprises, the records of mortuaries, the remnants of lending libraries, and the files of neighborhood hospitals and clinics come readily to mind.

My point in all of this is to illustrate the great difficulty we face in getting a full intellectual grasp of the categories of sources that could be considered "documentation of the immigrant experience." This problem manifests itself in more practical terms when decisions need to be made about collecting priorities based on the quality of different types of records and when procedures have to be devised for meeting varying preservation and access demands posed by diverse sources and media. Tackling these issues at the institutional level is bad enough; confronting them on a national or international scale seems frightening.

The fact that this material is presented in a multitude of languages further complicates matters. Historically, the inability of many archivists and librarians to read foreign language material contributed to the indifference and neglect that began to come to light in the 1960s. Today, the problem is perhaps less severe, but language is still affecting progress in documenting immigration. Cataloging projects involving non-English language material are generally more complex and costly, recruiting staff who combine suitable technical skills with language proficiency is still difficult for some language groups, and a number of repositories that hold immigration-related sources but do not specialize in that subject are, I suspect, still tending to set aside collecting and processing of documentation that staff cannot comprehend or evaluate. I also presume, but could never prove, that language deficiencies continue to play a role in decisions by private citizens and organizations to discard old papers of ancestors and predecessors. While many of the issues we address at this conference are common to historical research and archival activity generally, the language factor sets us apart from the mainstream, and we need to keep it in focus in our deliberations and plans.

The obstacle I want to call to our attention last is one that is not unique to the arena of immigration history but is possibly more pronounced here than in other fields. I would argue that there is a prevailing modus operandi of isolationism in regard to the relationship of repositories to each other as well as to their researchers. It is true, as Rudy has said, that various archival institutions cooperate in some ways informally. But this happens quite rarely, on the whole, and we seem to lack the motivation to take fuller advantage of collaborative opportunities or to create them. Is it because we are simply too busy keeping our own ships afloat, or are there other forces at work such as proprietary or overly competitive impulses, ethnocentrism, or basic lack of interest in the bigger picture?

I believe that limited resources *is* the chief explanation, but if any kinds of attitudinal constraints do exist, we had better confront them openly if we are to find ways to work together. In the case of relations between researchers and archivists or librarians, this conference itself serves to illustrate my point. Meetings that bring together researchers and information specialists to discuss, in unison and not separately, a scholarly publication project and documentation issues are very uncommon. This partnership seems as though it should be natural, but it needs persistent cultivation. The two groups simply don't understand each other well, and we seldom communicate outside the context of specific research inquiries and visits.

As much as we would like to dismiss it, I think there are still some unhealthy stereotypes to be found in either camp toward the other. Should we unravel all of this in the next two days? No, I don't believe so; we need to be looking forward more than backward. But I do feel that we need at least to acknowledge that a cohesive, collegial relationship among the users and keepers of immigrant documentation is not now in place. Its establishment, which is crucial to progress in my opinion, will not happen automatically.

This preceding litany of obstructions is, of course, far from complete. However, I now want to turn to the task of searching for the pathway out of our maze. I have not found this pathway; I'm not yet even sure it really exists. However, I do have some random thoughts on what the right track might look like, as do, I'm sure, all of you. The pooling of these ideas in our forthcoming workshops is what I look forward to most in this conference.

Possible Solutions: Efforts Underway

If there is a correct path, I would expect it to be marked with footprints. We are not the first to set out on this kind of a journey, and there are undoubtedly some lessons to be learned from these other endeavors. In 1983, a group of Canadian archivists, historians, and others met in Toronto at what was called the "Ethnic Archives Workshop." The stated purpose of the meeting was "to conduct a general investigation into the state of ethnic archives in Canada and to explore ways of improving them." The group discussed a number of the issues that Rudy, John, and I have alluded to and issued a set of recommendations to which I will refer again as I continue.[6] Unfortunately, I did not obtain any information on follow-up activities from the conference; I hope a few of you might know something of this.

In the United States, a recent gathering to explore archival documentation of American evangelical history included an agenda and mixture of participant perspectives not too different from ours. The published report from this event has helped to inform some of my comments, and we have with us Bob Shuster, the meeting's coordinator, to share more detailed observations.[7] Also, the Labor Archives Roundtable of the Society of American Archivists has been exploring with some energy the matter of coordinated collection development and has conducted survey work on labor-related archival holdings in the United States. Kenneth Fones Wolf may have more to tell us about how these efforts have progressed.

Of course, some of our best precedents and models reside in our own backyards. The Balch Institute is in the midst of an intensive collecting effort involving ethnic organizational records in the Delaware Valley, and it has a history of extraordinary success in attracting foundation support for acquisition and cataloging work.[8] The Center for Migration Studies has laid the groundwork for developing a comprehensive thesaurus of subject terms pertaining to migration, an outcome that could contribute significantly to standardization of cataloging practices and inter-institutional communication. The Mexican American Archives at the University of Texas received an NEH grant this year to enter its manuscript collection descriptions into one of the national bibliographic networks.

The IHRC will be undertaking similar work this year when it transforms its microcomputer database of archival cataloging records to the Research Libraries Information Network (RLIN) system. In addition, the IHRC's recent three-year Sons of Italy Archives Project and its extensive collection analysis effort, both supported in part by NHPRC, serve as instructive case studies of collection development planning and implementation.[9] These kinds of experiences should provide a source of light along the path if we can foster an exchange of insights at this conference and subsequently.

John has relayed some of the current developments in the archival profession that will play a part in shaping the work we do after this meeting. I want to amplify just a few of these briefly. No one has developed a precise formula for determining what documentation ought to be acquired and why; no one ever will or should. But the trend toward more deliberate, rationalized judgment in collecting has undeniable relevance for the field of immigration, given the various obstacles I outlined above. Although extreme doses of structure and strategy could, as I see it, render the *process* of collecting a higher goal than the collecting itself, a moderate injection would be healthy, at both the institution and multi-institution levels. I find myself agreeing with Joe Anderson and others who suggest that the best framework for collection building is one that sets down clear guidelines but also accommodates unforeseen opportunities and changing realities.[10] A fixed plan or policy is not what we should be striving for within our own institutions or in any cooperative ventures we undertake. But as one colleague put it, "Archivists do not need to hear another disclaimer that collecting is, after all, more art than science. Even an art form demands rigor, attention to detail, and some rationale for the technique."[11]

With regard to archival preservation and access developments, the key point to remember is that there are methods and activities in place with which we can connect: there *are* national computer networks (RLIN and OCLC) for cataloging primary source material as well as books. These networks are accessible to researchers and already contain a wealth of archival data, though you won't yet find too much information on most of the major repositories of immigration material. There *is* a national program for preserving and cataloging newspapers, the NEH U.S. Newspaper Microfilm Project.[12] This effort is beginning to make some headway in incorporating the ethnic press, but it has a long, long way to go in that direction. There *is* a continually growing body of literature on various other kinds of preservation problems and solutions, and there is currently a great deal of research and thought being devoted to standardization of archival descriptive practices.[13] (The technical process of cataloging archival material in the national networks is essentially standardized already.)

In addition, there are ongoing consortium-based projects involving preservation microfilming and automated cataloging of manuscript collections. Then, too, the commercial microfilm publishing industry is showing signs of growth and has clearly been targeting immigration-related material for filming and distribution.[14]

All of this is relevant to improving the state of documentation on immigration. Our conference should serve as the starting point for sorting out just how these developments can best be applied to our individual and collective needs.

Possible Solutions: New Initiatives

I want to conclude with a short list of actions I would like to see transpire after this conference, grouped under the rubrics of "communication," "coordination," and "experimentation." A common thread can be found in nearly all of my preceding remarks: we simply do not know very much about who has what kind of documentation and what they are doing with it, and we do not have enough information about who actually uses this material and with what results.

Improved communication is perhaps the one best outcome we could produce, and toward that end, I recommend that we devise some type of newsletter devoted to the collection, preservation, and use of historical documentation on immigration. Who would edit it? Distribute it? Finance it? Should it be produced independently or as part of another circular, such as the Immigration History Society Newsletter, where more researchers are apt to pay attention to it? These are sticky details, but worth resolving for the sake of having a convenient tool for sharing helpful information.

One of the recommendations of the Canadian Ethnic Archives Workshop called for another kind of communication device—a comprehensive, updatable directory of repositories related to ethnic history. The Evangelical Archives conference reached a similar conclusion. It makes sense to me for our situation also. We have some useful precedents upon which to build, but they are now either somewhat dated, such as the Wynar/Buttlar *Guide to Ethnic Museums, Libraries, and Archives*, or less comprehensive than we might prefer, as with the Center for Migration Studies' *Directory of International Migration Study Centers, Research Programs, and Library Resources*.[15] While I see a new, more inclusive directory as potentially very worthwhile for the keepers, users, *and* donors of archival material, I do see it as a pretty enormous task, and I think we should carefully consider its probable costs and benefits in relationship to other desireable efforts, such as promoting more extensive cataloging in the national computer networks.

My firmest conviction about this conference and its aftermath is that in order for any real progress to be made, we have to constitute some kind of coordinating entity that will continue to meet and to stimulate cooperative activity. This, too, was a recommendation of the 1983 Canadian conference, although I am not aware if it was ever enacted. We have all been to our share of conferences that promise new beginnings but lead nowhere; because of this, I've had more than a few fits of skepticism throughout the planning process for this event.

What purpose would such a coordinating group serve? Along with generally sustaining whatever momentum is realized here, I would see it performing three major functions: 1) attacking the problem of limited resources by finding ways for repositories to consolidate what little they do have and by soliciting new revenue for cooperative projects (again, I do believe there is money out there to meet some of our needs); 2) serving as a clearinghouse of information and perhaps advice for the multitude of people who have something to do with documenting the immigrant experience; and 3) solidifying partnerships among repositories and between the repositories and their constituents.

This last point raises the question of representation, and I want to stress something that Rudy mentioned. The number of institutions within the ethnic communities that hold historical collections is far greater than that of academic or private research centers such as the Immigration History Research Center. Their perspective must be prominent in any collaborative decision making, as must be the perspectives of those who *use* documentation for a variety of purposes. Just how we go about forming a coordinating body I do not know. But I am convinced that we cannot go far from here without it.

Under the heading of experimentation, I'd like to recommend that we do more collecting. While the idea of collecting might not seem experimental, doing some of it in a truly collaborative fashion would be. I think the archival world generally—and not only the immigration history sector—is undergoing a period of relative inactivity in acquiring new documentation. This is admittedly impressionistic, based partly on my own institution's situation, in which storage space and other factors demanded a slowing down of the impressive pace set in the late 60s and 70s.

I would like to see some concrete multi-institutional acquisition initiatives emerge in the near future. Might there be developed, for example, an archival version of the recent Cleveland ethnic history research project coordinated by Dirk Hoerder? New York, the country's largest concentration of previous and current immigrants, is still, I think, underdocumented with respect to this subject and might be a logical target site. Such an adventure would not need to be geographically based. Within some ethnic groups, repositories have already reached certain informal understandings about dividing collecting turf. The work of the United Fund for Finnish American Archives and the Greek American Historical Documents Project represent more concerted efforts to apply cohesiveness to these relationships and thereby facilitate cooperative acquisition and preservation work.[16] Perhaps these or other similar programs could serve as building blocks for a proactive collecting initiative.

72

A cooperative acquisition project not only would add new research material to archives, it could enable us to wrestle with the many issues I've raised on a more manageable scale than our conference furnishes. Choosing, planning, and implementing any such project will be exceedingly difficult. But let's not let the complications drown our creativity—this conference should be viewed as an opportunity to air fresh ideas as well as proven experiences.

My final suggestion echoes Rudy's comments about the larger role we play in advancing society's understanding of its multicultural character. Our deliberations will be worth most if we remember that this meeting is not simply about documents, research, and publication projects. Historian David McCollough concluded a recent PBS documentary profile of Frank Popiołek, a 90-year-old Polish immigrant living in Chicago, with the following words:

> Memories are short and getting shorter, unfortunately. In many families, the years before the 2nd World War are fast fading; the time before the first War—Frank Popiołek's time—is gone, as remote as Caesar. Alone playing solitaire, Frank Popiołek is not just a man from another distant place, but from a vastly different time, which counts heavily in his loneliness. If we stop to think of how much emotion, how much of real and irreplaceable value in our lives comes from the past, then maybe we'll not be so quick to discard it and all those who go with it.[17]

The work we do ought to serve the ultimate purpose of moving people toward this greater appreciation of the past. When we can tell ourselves that this purpose has been fulfilled, I think we will know we've found our way through the archival maze.

Notes

1.   Joel Wurl, "Research and Information Centers in Migration Studies," in Eva Sartori, et al., *Western European Studies: Current Research Trends and Library Resources*, (Chicago: Association of College and Research Libraries, Western European Specialists Section, Occasional Publication No. 3, 1990).

2.   S. B. Vardy and Agnes Huszar Vardy, "Historical, Literary, Linguistic, and Ethnographic Research on Hungarian Americans: A Historiographical Assessment," *Hungarian Studies* 1 (1985).

3. Perhaps the most forceful advocate for a proactive perspective in archival acquisition has been F. Gerald Ham, former Wisconsin state archivist. See particularly "The Archival Edge," *American Archivist* 38 (January 1975), 5-13, "Archival Strategies for the Post-Custodial Era," *American Archivist* 44 (Summer 1981), 207-216, and "Archival Choices: Managing the Historical Record in the Age of Abundance," *American Archivist* 47 (Winter 1984), 11-22. Deliberate planning decision making are integral to the "documentation strategy" model, a recently articulated framework for developing archival holdings. Among the relevant writings on this theme are Helen Willa Samuels, "Who Controls the Past, *American Archivist* 49 (Spring 1986), 109-24, and Larry Hackman and Joan Warnow-Blewett, "The Documentation Strategy Process: A Model and A Case Study," *American Archivist* 50 (Winter 1987), 12-47.

4. Lubomyr Wynar and Lois Buttlar, *Ethnic Museums, Libraries, and Archives in the United States* (Kent, OH: Kent State University Press, 1978).

5. Victor Greene, "E. Pinkowski, Lay Collector; A Neglected Historical Resource," *Journal of American Ethnic History* 8 (Fall 1988), 10-20.

6. The findings of this conference are summarized in Elizabeth Boghossian, *Ethnic Archives Workshop Report*, (Ottawa: Minister of Supply and Services, 1985).

7. *A Heritage at Risk: The Proceedings of the Evangelical Archives Conference, July 13-15, 1988*, (Wheaton, IL: Billy Graham Center, Wheaton College, 1988).

8. This project is described in the spring and fall 1990 issues of the Institute's newsletter, *New Dimensions*.

9. The development and results of these projects are described in Joel Wurl and Lynda DeLoach, *Immigration History Research Center Report to the Collection Development Advisory Committee* (St. Paul: IHRC, 1988); and John Andreozzi, comp., *Guide to the Records of the Order Sons of Italy in America* (St. Paul: IHRC, 1989).

10. R. Joseph Anderson, "Managing Change and Chance: Collecting Policies in Social History Archives," *American Archivist* 48 (Summer 1985), 296-303.

11. Virginia R. Stewart, "A Primer on Manuscript Field Work," *Midwestern Archivist* 1 (1976), 4.

12. The goals and policies of the USNP are described in National Endowment for the Humanities, Office of Preservation, *Guidelines and Application Instructions*, (Washington: 1990), 14-16.

13. The *American Archivist* devoted nearly two full issues (52:4, Fall 1989; and 53:1, Winter 1990) to the report and background papers produced by an ad hoc Working Group on Standards for Archival Description.

14. Two examples of this interest are the "Immigrant in America" microfilm series produced by Research Publications, Woodbridge, Connecticut, and the "Research Collections in American Immigration" series produced by University Publications of America, Bethesda, Maryland.

15. Lubomyr Wynar and Lois Buttlar, *Ethnic Museums, Libraries, and Archives in the United States* (Kent, OH: Kent State University Press, 1978) and *A Directory of International Migration Study Centers, Research Programs, and Library Resources* (Staten Island: Center for Migration Studies, 1987).

16. These projects are described in two brochures: *A Guide to Collecting and Preserving Finnish American History: A Message from the United Fund for Finnish American Archives* (Minneapolis: United Fund for Finnish American Archives); and *The Greek-American Historical Documents Project: Preserving the Greek-American Past for the Future* (New York: Center for Byzantine and Modern Greek Studies, Queens College, CUNY).

17. "God Bless America and Poland, Too," *The American Experience* television documentary series, PBS, 1990 (available from PBS Video, Alexandria, Virginia).

Hunting the Snark; or, The Historian's Quest for Immigrant Documentation

Kathleen Neils Conzen

Lewis Carroll's Baker understood well the technique for hunting the Snark.

"If your Snark be a Snark, that is right," he observed,

> "'You may seek it with thimbles—and seek it with care;
> You may hunt it with forks and hope;
> You may threaten its life with a railway-share;
> You may charm it with smiles and soap—'"

But he also realized that to hunt the Snark was to risk a terrible fate:

> "'But oh, beamish nephew, beware of the day,
> If your Snark be a Boojum! For then
> You will softly and suddenly vanish away,
> And never be met with again!'"[1]

The Baker's warnings to would-be Snark-hunters have special resonance to a historian like me, who has been engaged off and on over the past fifteen years—sometimes intensively, sometimes with long periods of distraction by other projects—in a seemingly interminable quest to document the experience of a particular group of immigrants at a particular place and time. My quarry are the several thousand German Catholic families who farmed in Stearns County, Minnesota, between 1854 and 1930, forming more than thirty Catholic parishes and coming to dominate the economic, social, and political life of the county, with consequences that remain evident today. Knowing why and how these families constructed a distinctive kind of culture in an area like Stearns County, I am arguing, not only clarifies the range of outcomes possible within the historical process of immigrant adaptation, but also helps explain the emotive bases of American family farming, the sources of one strain of American Catholicism, and the logic of one particular brand of American political behavior.[2]

My quest has had its idiosyncracies. In its focus upon a so-called "older" immigrant group, on one that has been very numerous and whose language stands some fair chance of being at least recognized by educated Americans, it may have avoided certain kinds of research problems endemic to the study of many other immigrant groups. On the other hand, the weak organizational base of German American ethnicity has lent little urgency to efforts at collection development. The rural focus of my work has also generated peculiar kinds of data problems and possibilities that the more common kind of urban immigrant study would not face. Still, my Stearns County research can serve, I hope, as a case study with which to illustrate some broader issues that users--whether as researchers or as teachers--face in documenting the immigrant experience, and that we might consider as we seek to formulate a national strategy for immigrant historical documentation. Lewis Carroll, I have come to realize, understood the perils of the quest for immigrant documentation only too well. In my case, I set out hunting a Snark, with the scholar's tried and true equivalent of thimbles, forks, and hope. I encountered a Boojum instead.

The basic problem lies in the historian's constantly expanding conception of the immigrant experience. When immigration history essentially comprised, as it did for the first generation of filiopietist historians, the achievements of notable group members, the task of documentation was simple: collect the papers of famous men and of the ethnic associations that they formed. This was the collecting agenda set by the early ethnic historical societies, and it is an agenda that many effectively maintain. But as attention has turned to the social history of immigration and the lives of all immigrants, as well as to the multi-generational evolution of ethnic cultures, the range of questions to be addressed has greatly broadened, and with it the types of sources that fall potentially within the historian's purview. The result is user demand for entirely new categories of documentation, and thus a research quest that must encompass not only traditional ethnic history collections but a wide range of public and private libraries and archives, governmental agencies, and "history on the ground," or the landscapes and artifacts constructed by the immigrants, as well as the "history in people's minds," or oral history.

Scholars have obviously not been content to let existing collections define the way they conceptualize their questions. Yet there are only too clearly limits to the degree to which archives can move to meet ever-shifting scholarly interests. Are there then ways in which we can better marshall our collection strategies and bibliographic resources to meet at least some of these needs? Previous speakers have focused most directly on the issues confronting archives that have explicitly ethnic collecting agendas. My own odyssey suggests certain other areas to which we must also direct our attention.

I began with a straightforward-enough research strategy. Stated in over-simplified terms, I decided to use linked manuscript censuses and land and tax records to lay out the basic parameters of local social and economic integration. I would then derive from them a sample group of immigrants to trace back to a homeland community, and I would use surviving newspapers and manuscript collections to illuminate the patterns thus found. But I soon encountered a range of problems. It became clear that the immigrants in question came from a dauntingly wide array of German home towns. The statistical patterns were clear, but their meaning and explanation could not be derived intuitively from the data analysis alone.

Local archives had minimal collections that would shed light on motives and categories of experience, and the county clerk was less than forthcoming in allowing access to local government records. There is no single major archival collection devoted to German Americana on a national basis, and my study area is in any case too far off the beaten ethnic track to attract much attention from such German American collections as do exist.

Under these circumstances, I decided simply to let the sleeping dog of Stearns County German Americana lie dormant a little longer while I turned to other matters. When I subsequently returned to the project, it was with a sharpened theoretical perspective that placed much more emphasis upon the process of cultural construction in America, and with a much more omnivorous appetite for data. In essence, I postulated an expanding set of circles within which cultural construction occurred—farm, family, neighborhood, parish, market community, nested local polities, etc.—and tried to determine for each the kinds of activities that might have left a paper trail, whether or not that paper trail might have survived, and if so, where it could be found. Most social historians, I suspect, work in similar fashion.[3]

Two unpredictable pieces of good fortune were responsible for whatever success I have had with this strategy. The first was the decision of the state of Minnesota to encourage counties to deposit in the state archives records that they no longer wished to keep, and the decision of Stearns County to be among the first to take advantage of this new policy. No longer was I to be cast upon the mercy of a pitiless county clerk; I had the pleasant and utterly professional services of the staff of the Minnesota Historical Society upon which to call. And the second was the decision of Stearns County to construct and support a Heritage Center that in both its physical facilities and in the strength and professionalization of its collections must be among the finest in the state. The degree to which the county's local historical awareness and pride has been generated from deeply subterranean roots over the last decade and a half has been truly remarkable, and owes a good deal, I suspect, to the national ethnic revival that has made coming out of the German American closet both respectable and desirable.

My other two pieces of good fortune were of longer standing and therefore more predictable but equally critical: the general excellence and significant ethnic emphasis of the collections of the Minnesota Historical Society, and the superb archival tradition of the Benedictines, which created at St. John's Abbey a complex and beautifully organized documentary record of the county's popular piety.

Rather than attempt to reconstruct here all the various paper trails that I followed in hunting my immigrants, let me just suggest some of the destinations to which they led. Some were quite far afield—Washington, D.C., for example. In the National Archives, I found homestead applications, where immigrants described the homes they had constructed and some of the circumstances of their farm-making. I found Indian Claims Commission reports, where immigrants described the homes they had lost in the Sioux Uprising of 1862. I found Civil War provost marshalls' reports, which documented widespread local draft dodging, and military records, which uncovered the sometimes farcical, frequently sad, and generally inglorious record of immigrant war service. Voluminous pension records testified not only to some of the lasting consequences of the war, but to innumerable details of daily life and aging. Sadly, however, since Stearns County was a hive of moonshining activity, Treasury Department reports on the local enforcement of the Volstead Act did not survive a 1950s archival housecleaning.

Microfilmed federal records, of course, have been equally central. They include not only the decennial censuses and their indexes, but also ship passenger lists, Indian agency papers, and territorial papers—the latter two sources invaluable in reconstructing the initial settlement history of the area.

My quest has led me to several other out-of-state and foreign collections as well. I have consulted the Dun and Co. credit rating reports of Stearns County businessmen in Harvard's Baker Library. The State Historical Society of Wisconsin harbors not only an important collection of immigrant letters and material relevant to the pre-Minnesota careers of some of the early Stearns County immigrants, but also fur traders' and politicians' papers that shed light on the area's early history. The archives of Michigan State University contain additional relevant personal papers of this kind.

Even more critical have been the genealogical collections of the Newberry Library and the Mormon Genealogical Library in Salt Lake City. Genealogical methods proved to be the only way to get some handle both on the origins of the immigrants and the paths that brought them to Minnesota, and on where they settled after they left Stearns County. The collections of these two libraries greatly eased my sample traces as well as my attempts to characterize the communities of origin and destination. Although the widely scattered origins of the Stearns County immigrant population, and my altered focus on the continuous process of local American cultural construction, worked against detailed European community reconstitution, I also dipped into the resources of the Prussian State Archives at Koblenz to consult emigration permits and some local community records.

But most of my paper trails stopped at Minnesota destinations. The cornucopia of riches at the Minnesota Historical Society alone could have kept me occupied for years. Critical for my entire project were the county civil and criminal case files for which the Society has provided a home. It is through these records that I have been able to hear numerous local residents speaking of their daily lives in their own voices, and that I have been able to find pattern in many of their public acts. Here also I consulted county probate records, records of local governments, naturalization records, local correspondence with the General Land Office in Washington, more Civil War and Sioux Uprising documentation, Public Safety Commission files, Non-Partisan League papers, and the like. Governors' papers yielded some particularly revealing letters from local residents. The Society's newspaper collection is rich in local German- as well as English-language files. And while there are virtually no papers from Stearns County German Americans in its collections, the papers of several local Anglo-Americans yielded important comparative material as well as insight into interethnic relations.

St. John's Abbey Archives was another treasure trove. The letters of early monks contain some of the very few first-person accounts of pioneer settlement. Parish files and priests' files present often dramatic documentation of the ways in which immigrants and clergy interacted in constructing parishes and their associated organizations and schools. The Abbots' papers present not only the formal concerns of the church, but also direct evidence of lay concerns in the streams of complaining and congratulatory letters that found their way from the countryside to the Abbey. Patterns of popular piety can be reconstructed as well from Mass announcement books, sermon collections, and even parish and pastoral accounts, while Benedictine efforts to follow—or lead—their flock further west provide documentation for certain patterns of out-migration. The manuscript autobiographies and family histories of monks raised in the area often offer perceptive, sophisticated analysis of local values. And because a late nineteenth-century Abbot was an avid photographer, there is a large collection of glass-plate negatives—including hundreds of wedding photos—for documenting the visual appearance of the early county.

The county's Heritage Center in St. Cloud does harbor a small number of immigrant diaries and letters, as well as large collections of WPA interviews (copies of which are also available at the Minnesota Historical Society), voluminous untranscribed oral history tapes, and subject-classified photograph files. Here also I have consulted extensive biographical folders for local residents (these contain mainly clippings from local newspapers), more local government documents, a growing collection of local genealogies, and the papers of a small number of local organizations that have been donated to the Center.

This accounting does not exhaust my odyssey. There are additional church and education records that I could note. Moreover, a local title company was extremely generous with its deeds records, and I suspect that a personal scouring of the county could turn up some critical collections of associational and business records that have yet to find their way into an archive. But I would completely exhaust your patience were I to carry on much further. I have said enough in any case, I hope, for you to begin to see the Boojum-esque quality of my Snark.

For the German immigrant whom I set out to find is also an everyday American; and virtually every source, and every archive, that can shed light on American social history also illuminates the immigrant condition. No collection can necessarily be ruled out in advance; declarations of archival turf offer little assistance. For how is one to specify that point where the immigrant stops and the ethnic American begins, or where ethnicity itself fades, or to separate those areas of life that can be said to be influenced by ethnicity from those that are not?

As Lewis Carroll's Snark-hunter moaned, "It is this, it is this that I dread." For

> "... if ever I meet with a Boojum, that day,
> In a moment (of this I am sure),
> I shall softly and suddenly vanish away--
> And the notion I cannot endure!"[4]

The social historian skirts perilously close to this fate, as I know to my sorrow, when he or she sets out to follow the immigrant's paper trail. Despite the explosion of information management tools within the archival profession in the last couple decades, and despite heroic recent efforts to document the ethnic dimension of American life, the user still confronts a chaotic jumble of sources and archives characterized by far too little in the way of coordinated collection strategies, bibliographic aids, or even full appreciation of the value of much of what they do have. This is one of those cases, I am sure we would all agree, where throwing significant amounts of money at the problem would do wonders for its alleviation. But my user's perspective also suggests several strategies short of that final nirvana with which we might begin.

Let me briefly discuss a number of general areas of concern, and then conclude with a few specific suggestions. The first area of concern that I would like to point to derives from my realization of the centrality of government documents to reconstructing the immigrant story. Immigration historians have long since made the manuscript census and ship arrival lists staples of their trade, but far fewer historians have made use of the array of public sources to which I was driven in the absence of more familiar kinds of documentation.

Some of this is undoubtedly owing to conceptual blinkers. Many of these sources, after all, show the immigrant in generic situations where his or her actions are those also engaged in by every other American, while the historian's concern is often to document the specifically ethnic. To the extent that we want to document ethnic autonomy, we turn our attention away from those areas of life—tax paying, politics, litigation, military service, welfare receipt, road building—where the limits of autonomy are quickly apparent, where an interethnic public sphere is of necessity constructed. And because the public sphere is not examined, the historian may then dismiss it as irrelevant.

In an area like Stearns County, this public sphere is hard to ignore, since the Germans themselves largely succeeded in constructing the rules governing behavior within it. But even in urban settings, the ways in which immigrant-stock Americans behaved in their public actions, and the paper trails left by their involvement with public agencies, are central to the documentation of their American lives.

But even the best-intentioned potential user can be frustrated by real difficulties of access. The clerk of court whom I encountered was surely not the only one to regard the idea of a historian pawing over the case files in her custody as a nuisance whom she could afford to do without. Privacy concerns also can close thousands of documents for fear of the one scandal that may emerge. Simple lack of information about the contents of government data sets can be equally inhibiting; the fifty-year-old W.P.A. guides to county, state, and church records generally remain the best means of access at our disposal. The National Archives are well-documented, but not in a fashion that immediately underlines their usefulness to the historian of the local ethnic community unless approached through the filter of family history or genealogy (a point to which I shall return). And—witness my attempt to track down the record of federal efforts to curb Stearns County moonshining—every historian has a tale to tell of public documents destroyed or misplaced.

Thus we must recognize that public records are as central a part of the documentation of the immigrant experience as personal papers or associational files. Indeed—if I may sound for the moment like an old "new social historian"—for many immigrants and their children they provide the only documentation. This means that we have to take an interest in their preservation and in insuring access to them. This may involve hard decisions as public archives become overwhelmed with paper.

An archivist asked me, for example, if my purposes could have been served equally well by a systematic sample of Stearns County district court case files; my answer was no. What then if they simply sampled counties—that is, agreed to preserve the case files for only a certain number of counties? Fine, but how to choose? If you save Stearns County for its Germans, what about Brown, with its equally interesting but different Germans? Or what about the Swedes of Chisago? Well then, why not the Swedes in Isanti? Or the Norwegians up in Pope, or the Poles in Benton, or the Luxemburgers in Winona, or the Slavs on the Range?

We have to work with local governments to help them recognize the value of their holdings, we have to work with public archivists on issues of preservation, access, and cataloguing, and we should insure that the value of these collections for immigration history is properly acknowledged in the guides for our own field that we write.

I might note parenthetically that we even have an interest in the details of collection arrangement. One of my greatest frustrations in doing research on Germans in early Milwaukee was the fact that although the county historical society had managed to preserve all the early probate files, it stored them alphabetically rather than chronologically, making their use virtually impossible for anything but genealogical purposes.

My second area of concern is closely related: We should draw church archives into similarly close cooperation. The secular orientation of most historians, the frequently close links between immigration historiography and radical labor historiography, the suspicion or decentralization or penury or impermanence of many of the churches themselves, have long contributed to a general underuse of church archives among many immigration historians. Yet it is one of the standard pieties of our field that the church was the only institution that immigrants were able to bring with them to America, and many American churches were long defined by their ethnic character. Moreover, church records, as I have discovered, can illuminate significant areas of immigrant life other than religion alone, including both family relationships and the community economy.

The access and bibliographic situation is now changing for the better, at least in the Catholic Church, that largest of immigrant churches, and both immigration historians and historians of religion are developing a new interest in modes of popular piety and participation. But there is much that can still be done. My own experience suggests that the records of lay societies are often underrepresented in church archives, whether at the parish or diocesan level, yet society officers can be reluctant to deposit them in a non-church-related institution. Can we encourage some kind of collecting strategy? What is happening to the records of the numerous small, often immigrant-founded religious institutions that fade from the scene each year? What about the church-linked insurance societies?

We should also encourage the collection of the artifacts of pre-Vatican II ethnic popular piety. Recently, for example, the Stearns County Heritage Center received as a donation one woman's lifetime collection of death cards—those devotional impedimenta that littered every Catholic's missal for decades. They preserve valuable demographic data, but even more important is the way in which they document the evolving contours of this pious practice, and the involvement of one woman in a complex, overlapping communal network of salvation. Surveys of ethnic material in church archives, similar to recent surveys of archival resources for the history of women religious, or of Catholic Indian missions, may be the most efficient way of bringing these resources to the attention of potential immigration history users.[5]

My Snark hunt also suggests a third area where such coordination is necessary and desirable: with local historical societies and libraries. In this context, the user faces two very different categories of problems. On the one hand, such repositories often are not interested in collecting ethnic material. They may have an origin and orientation that blinds them to the historical significance of their area's ethnic heritage; or more prosaically, they may lack the language skills to properly evaluate ethnic materials that may be offered to them. A query to an out-of-state county historical society regarding a set of German diaries mentioned in a recently-published history of the county may meet with the curt reply that the history of the county's German Catholics is none of their concern. Another county historical society may operate an impressive pioneer village that is filled with structures built by German Lutherans who settled in one half of the county, but that totally ignores the German-speaking Catholics who dominated the other.

The new grass-roots interest in ethnic community and family history is affecting these societies, and encouraging many to expand their collecting scope. But this raises a second set of problems. If a formerly elitist local institution, for example, sets out to expand its ethnic focus, might it not then siphon off potential collections from local ethnic group archives that had been established to counter the previous indifference of that same elitist institution? Yet if ethnic material does not play an important role in historical society collections, how can local users be blamed if they do not include immigrants in the histories they construct?

At the same time, as more ethnic material finds its way into local collections, how is the scholar to be made aware of its availability? Few have the resources to publish collection guides, or contribute descriptions of their collections to national data bases. Many, indeed, function with neither professional staffs nor adequate storage facilities or cataloging for the collections that they have been given, so that invaluable records documenting the Germanization of a local public school district, for example, may lie gathering dust in an unheated schoolhouse museum staffed with volunteers on summer Sunday afternoons; or the preservation of donated diaries and letters may depend on the good will and conscience of a society's secretary who keeps them in her home and remembers to pass them on to her successor after she leaves office.

There is an enormous level of good will and historical interest among the members of such societies, and many states have effective programs to assist in their professionalization. But any national strategy for collecting, preserving, and making more accessible the documentation of our immigrant heritage must also take them into account. An active local society is often the repository-of-first-resort for community residents with family papers or associational records to donate.

Previous speakers have noted the surprising lack of diaries and letters in many ethnically-defined archives. Many more of these sources, I suspect, are to be found in local societies closer to home, where families can retain a sense of access. This is particularly the case where an ethnic group is well-integrated into its local community, a situation that is becoming ever more common. How can these local societies be better assisted in managing their collections? How can we better spread the word about the contents of their collections?

This leads me to a set of specific concluding suggestions to help alleviate the Snark-hunting risks of immigration history research. Simply inventorying what is already available in various kinds of collections seems the first priority. We know that most smaller and local archives will not be able to afford to list their holdings in on-line or published databases. But would it be possible to stimulate more descriptive surveys of immigration-related holdings in collections in particular localities or states? Such surveys could highlight significant local materials that might also be of interest to users on a broader level—particularly rich diaries or associational records, collections of photographs or artifacts, oral history collections, and the like.

Here—as in other areas, I might observe—we should pursue cooperation with genealogists, who have often taken the lead in this kind of endeavor, and who provide one of the largest users' markets for such surveys.[6] Since such area surveys, when they are produced, are often rather irregular in their form of publication and distribution, it would also help to have a continuously-updated bibliography of immigration-related area collection guides and where they can be consulted.

Secondly, are there additional programs that could be developed to increase the sensitivity of local historical societies and church archives to ethnic materials, and most importantly, to make available to them language specialists who could assist in evaluating, cataloguing, and arranging foreign-language collections? As mother tongue familiarity fades, this problem will increase, even for materials in languages that use the Roman alphabet. Many German manuscripts, for example, are not only in a foreign language, but in an unfamiliar script. The St. John's Abbey Archives has employed generations of retired monks in transcribing German script into familiar typescript, but the bulk of their material remains untranscribed, and few local archives have had such resources available. I suspect that the inability of many to read even the printed Gothic type has contributed to the disappearance of large amounts of published German Americana from library collections around the country.

Thirdly, would it make sense to develop some kind of policy statement or guide on the preservation of ethnically sensitive local government records? This is as much a matter of raising our own consciousness about the significance of these records as it is a matter of influencing local government officials themselves. It also involves working on policies for the public documentation of contemporary immigration.

A final set of suggestions concerns iconographic sources. Archives of all kinds are collecting more photographic and other iconographic sources than ever before, and historians are learning to use them not just for illustration but also for analysis. However, photographic collections are often not indexed for their value in interpreting ethnic communities unless clearly ethnic customs and costumes are depicted. Are there ways to encourage better analysis and reporting of major collections in terms of their ethnic relevance? Do we need much more specifically targetted collecting of photographic images to insure documentation of a wide range of immigrant cultures and activities?

Documenting the ethnic experience has posed special problems because of the long-perceived marginality of immigrant populations, the limited archival tradition within many ethnic groups, and the languages in which so many of the sources are written. We now have a much wider range of institutions interested in collecting the documents of the immigrant experience than ever before, and as the other speakers have indicated, we are now faced with important issues of collection development and coordination, preservation, and bibliographic control. Strategies for coping with these issues will be an important part of any project designed to make more of this documentation immediately available to other scholars, students, and the general public in a documentary history project.

But we have to remember also that the issue of ethnicity runs through virtually every kind of documentary record that Americans have produced. The more we keep the full range of these sources in mind, the better our chances of interpreting the ethnic experience as central to the interpretation of American history itself. And the more we improve our intellectual access to the full range of these repositories, the more we lessen the risk of historians "softly and suddenly vanishing away" when they set out to pursue their immigrant quarry.

Notes

1. "The Hunting of the Snark," *The Collected Verse of Lewis Carroll* (New York: E. P. Dutton & Co., 1929), 40-41.

2. For aspects of this argument, see Kathleen Neils Conzen, "Peasant Pioneers: Generational Succession among German Farmers in Frontier Minnesota," in Steven Hahn and Jonathan Prude, eds., *The Countryside in the Age of Capitalist Transformation: Essays in the Social History of Rural America* (Chapel Hill: University of North Carolina Press, 1985), 259-92; and Kathleen Neils Conzen, "Making Their Own America: Assimilation Theory and the German Peasant Pioneer," Annual Lecture Series, No. 3, German Historical Institute, Washington, D.C. (New York: Berg Publishers, 1990).

3. See, for example, the superb documentation, including oral history, that underlies Gary R. Mormino and George E. Pozzetta, *The Immigrant World of Ybor City: Italians and Their Latin Neighbors in Tampa, 1885-1985* (Urbana: University of Illinois Press, 1990), to cite only one of many possible examples.

4. Carroll, "Hunting of the Snark," 41.

5. Evangeline Thomas, *Women Religious History Sources: A Guide to Repositories in the United States* (New York: R. R. Bowker Company, 1983); Philip C. Bantin with Mark G. Thiel, *Guide to Catholic Indian Mission and School Records in Midwest Repositories* (Milwaukee: Department of Special Collections and University Archives, Marquette University, 1984).

6. For an excellent example of this kind of publication, see Loretto Dennis Szucs, *Chicago and Cook County Sources: A Genealogical and Historical Guide* (Salt Lake City, 1986).

In Their Own Words: Why Historians Need a Documentary History of the Immigrant Experience

Alan M. Kraut

The poet and physician William Carlos Williams once wrote, "I used to learn so much from the families I saw on my house calls—so much that I often wondered whose words I was putting into my poems, theirs or mine. Of course, we had no tape recorders, then. But I wrote down what I heard, carefully, after I'd leave. The problem later is artistic—what to use and where."[1]

These words echo the dilemma of modern historians who study society from the bottom up and who have available to them tape recorders and other state-of-the art technology. Which words are the correct ones to quote? Which descriptions the most vivid? How can we best convey the thoughts and feelings and lives of those who individually did not leave a substantial body of letters and diaries? And what do we do with the personal testimony we have?

Such questions have perennially perplexed historians of immigration to the United States. Building upon the poetic, if somewhat obscure portrait of uprooted wanderers presented by Oscar Handlin during the 1950s, immigration historians have added the more complex and varied realities of specific groups coming to the United States, not just from Europe, but from Asia, Africa, and Latin America. Inspired by the civil rights movement of the 1960s, the "ethnic revival" and search for roots in the 1970s, a new generation of scholars has brought the history of immigrants from Ireland, Italy, Greece, Russia, Poland, China, Japan, and the Caribbean into the American intellectual mainstream. And there has been marked progress.

In a 1970 article our colleague and conference host Rudolph Vecoli proclaimed ethnicity "a neglected dimension of American history."[2] In his presidential address to the Immigration History Society fifteen years later, Vecoli celebrated "the burgeoning of ethnic and immigration history in the seventies" and a "younger generation of historians" who set out to document the experiences of the inarticulate, the powerless, the subaltern elements in American history; to understand the consciousness of workers, immigrant women and blacks; to perceive the world through their eyes; to interpret their behavior through their values."

91

Especially impressive to Vecoli and to others was how much of this fresh scholarship was "free of pieties and orthodoxies." He praised its "sensitivity to the peculiarities of ethnic group experiences."[3] There is no better way to "perceive the world through their eyes" than to allow immigrants to speak across the generations in their own words, as translated from the languages they spoke when they arrived. An active international scholarly community is already studying immigration to America from the many perspectives of the donor society, the host society, the ethnic group, and the individual newcomer. At present, there are several anthologies that offer to students and scholars a sampling of documents, many of them originally in English, pertaining to immigration.[4] Other volumes offer translations of poetry and prose that convey the inner thoughts and feelings of newcomers.[5]

In one volume, young Chinese scholars have translated moving poems that Chinese immigrants carved in the walls of San Francisco's Angel Island immigration depot as they awaited the decision that would admit or exclude them. Expressing anxiety over the medical examination of newcomers, one such immigrant poet wrote:

It is indeed pitiable the harsh treatment of our fellow countrymen.
The doctor extracting blood caused us the greatest anguish.
Our stomachs are full of grievances, but to whom can we tell them?
We can but pace to and fro, scratch our heads, and question the blue sky.[6]

Such volumes are helpful, even inspiring, but insufficient. We cannot truly appreciate the immigrant experience so long as we must rely on scattered fragments of the immigrant story.

Granted, a documentary history looms as an especially formidable challenge. Differences of language among immigrants have made it difficult if not impossible for any one scholar to rely upon untranslated primary sources to treat a wide variety of different groups. Distinctions of culture and tradition among the newcomers makes yet more complicated and problematical the task of generalizing about the values, attitudes, and institutions of immigrants from many lands.

One solution to the scholar's dilemma is clearly to continue to produce narrow monographs on particular groups written by those who know the language and have developed a particular expertise and perhaps also an empathy for the group that is the focus of their scholarship. A second possibility is to rely on documents such as those in the National Archives, state and municipal archives, and the repositories of private voluntary organizations that provide information about immigrants whose lives touched or were touched by state or private institutions in this country. A brilliantly executed example of the latter is *Freedom: A Documentary History of Emancipation, 1861-1867*, Ira Berlin's documentary history of African Americans whose forebears had been the victims of forced migration. Berlin and his associates tapped the rich resources of many collections in the National Archives to allow black people to speak across time about becoming free. However, for the sake of manageability, the study was limited to materials in the National Archives. Therefore, much valuable testimony was of necessity excluded, especially resources generated by scattered slave and freedman communities describing the internal life of African-Americans.[7]

One of the projects undertaken by the Statue of Liberty/Ellis Island History Committee has been to study the feasibility of a multi-volume series of documentary histories of the immigrant experience. Such a series would allow scholars detailed treatment of particular groups' experiences, while placing those experiences within the context of the vastly heterogenous character of American immigration. The fresh cache of heretofore untranslated, untapped sources used in these volumes would immeasurably enrich our understanding of both immigrants' lives and their impact upon the United States.

It is important to emphasize that a documentary history of American immigration can never be undertaken in isolation from related concerns, especially the collecting, accessioning, and preservation of sources, which is the larger subject of this conference. However, before such a monumental project is launched, there must be a clear vision of the topical and chronological sweep of the series. Since 1986, the Statue of Liberty/Ellis Island History Committee has worked with immigration historians to develop a blueprint for a documentary history series. Victor Greene of the University of Wisconsin, Milwaukee, archivist Bara Levin, and I took the lead in the early stages of planning for the History Committee. Later, historian John Jentz and many others, including Mary Giunta and Nancy Sahli of the NHPRC, contributed their thoughts.

This is a report on the current state of the planning and discussion. It reflects discussion of some issues involved in laying the floor plan for a documentary history series and some of the preliminary decisions of those who have already been involved in the dialogue. It is a project still very much at the beginning.

Most of those involved in the early discussions of a documentary history series have preferred that it be organized by immigrant group rather than thematically. While all involved recognized the need for comparative approaches to the study of immigration and ethnicity, the difficulties of compiling volumes on a thematic basis have thus far appeared insurmountable. Also, a thematic approach with one or more volumes per theme would fragment the distinctive experience of each immigrant group and render a less effective research tool. Instead, a cumulative index to all of the volumes could be developed to promote comparative studies.

The rationale for the group approach is threefold. First, such an approach would simplify editorial control over the contents. Each volume editor would presumably be an expert on a particular group and have the necessary language skills to understand documents in that group's native tongue, making a staff of translators unnecessary. A second rationale is that each editor would already know many of the sources from which documents might be collected and assembled. Finally, this approach would allow for a complex grasp of the nuances and inter-relationships in group experiences that might well elude a single editor reviewing many groups simultaneously.

But which immigrant groups should be included? The definition of the term "immigrant group" is critical to establishing criteria for selection. Here one encounters difficult and controversial questions of nomenclature. Immigrants who arrived with quite specific localized identities (e.g. Swabians, Calabrians), were often gradually absorbed into larger ethnic groups (e.g. Germans and Italians). Immigrants from multinational empires such as Austria-Hungary included many distinctive nationalities (e.g. Slovaks, Magyars, Croatians), while certain once stateless nationalities (e.g. Ukrainians, Armenians) have become persistent ethnic groups in the United States and now appear never to have been as thoroughly absorbed by the Soviet Union as Soviet leaders claimed during the Cold War.

Those of us doing the initial planning proposed that the working definition of an "immigrant group" might be that of a group which emerged distinctly in this country after the consolidation of many smaller provincial groupings. These groups ought to be distinguishable from each other by language, culture, religion, race, or combinations of these characteristics. We thought that groups identified in the *Harvard Encyclopedia of American Ethnic Groups* might be used as a starting point, although we realized that this source of categories has been criticized for omitting some groups and for combining others somewhat arbitrarily. An alternative is using those designations that groups applied to themselves, as indicated by fraternal orders or other social groupings (e.g. The Sons of Italy).

Another issue and one related to the choice of groups is the chronological period that the project will cover. All of American history from 1600 to the present? The era from 1830 to 1930 that some call the Atlantic migration? The Ellis Island era, 1892 to 1954? In the end, a great many preliminary planners favored all of American history, but this question remains very much open for discussion.

Assuming that at some point there could be agreement on which groups and which era would be treated in the documentary history series, there remains still another large issue: what should be the nature of the documents included? Believing that such a series should not only view the immigrant experience from the bottom up, but from the "inside out," as well, Victor Greene and I early on pushed for the notion that the topics ought to reflect the internal life of the groups to be studied. Thus, the series would be less concerned with issues generated by national, state, or federal agencies and more focused upon issues generated by the immigrants themselves. These might include:

1) Migration and Settlement, treating the experience of leaving Europe and settling in America, including the secondary settlement that occurred when immigrant groups moved from older and more established ethnic communities to establish or join newer ones.

2) Earning a Living, dealing with the group's work experiences, job recruitment and the activities of entrepreneurs in the groups.

3) Governing and being governed, covering how groups sought political stability through the formation of ethnic institutions responsible for internal governance. This section of some volumes might also deal with urban political machines and the immigrant left.

4) Building Communities, dealing with the formation of ethnic leadership and the organizations they led. Editors might also include documents on the role of churches as institutions in various ethnic communities.

5) Worshipping, stressing the cultural aspects of religion, not the role of religious institutions in building communities.

6) Family and Home, providing demographic material on the specific group. This category might also include a discussion of child-rearing practices and inter-generational conflict between immigrant parents and their more assimilated children. There is a need for material on aging, as well as the changing roles of men and women after immigration.

7) Creating Cultural Forms, treating the immigrant group's role in American popular, folk, mass, and high culture. Under this rubric there might also be discussions of the groups' varied culture and

how distinctive patterns of speech and dress changed after immigration.

8) Caring institutions, taking up the interactions with American welfare, philanthropic, medical, and penal institutions from the immigrant perspective.

9) Learning, covering both publicly supported and private educational institutions.

10) Becoming Americans, recalling the immigrants' perceptions of Americanization as they were in the midst of it. Oral histories might be an especially valuable source here.

Of course, these are only suggestions; and individual editors would arrange treatment of their group according to the unique encounter which that group had with American society and the editor's own interpretive model.

That interpretive model, or the perspective of the editor upon the group, would exert a significant influence upon the shape of specific volumes. Few of the initial series planners wanted to interfere with editorial prerogative. Let me give you an example of the parameters envisioned.

As the title implies, *German Workers in Chicago: A Documentary History of Working-Class Culture in Chicago from 1850 to World War I* (1988) edited by Harmut Keil and John Jentz focuses upon the culture of a particular class. However, as the editors explain, "working-class culture was embedded in lower-class lifestyles and in a folk culture from which it drew many significant ways and with which it had much in common. It is therefore impossible to conceive of working-class culture except in relation to these other cultural traditions and ways of life: a rejection of them would have been equivalent to its own demise."[8] Keil and Jentz thus make the very crucial point that cultural traditions, if treated with the appropriate sensitivity to their origins and implications, must of necessity be described in their full breadth and interconnectedness. A similar awareness would be essential to a documentary on the immigration experience.

As for the kind of documents that might be used in the series, everyone who has participated in the discussion has agreed upon the broadest possible range, avoiding where possible all official documents in favor of letters, diary entries, newspaper articles from the immigrant press, poetry, songs, and all genre of documents that permit the voice of the immigrants to be heard most directly and with the fewest possible mediating voices. Then there is the problem of non-traditional sources. Some immigrants were illiterate and most immigrants recorded their presence in ways other than traditional written forms of self-expression. It was the opinion of early planners that the project should definitely treat non-documentary sources. But which ones and how? Some non-written sources that come to mind are photos, music, movies. Ought editors be encouraged to include photographic essays in volumes? How might we capture the significance of musical performances or dance forms? Could discographies be included in volume appendices? And, more generally, how might computer technology be used to preserve the sights and sounds of immigrant groups' cultural expressions? These are thorny problems with which scholars must wrestle.

Finally, those who have been involved in the early stages of planning this series have been quite firm in their resolve that the end product should be documentary histories and not merely collections of documents. Each volume, however many of them there are, must present extensive introductory material and commentary. In format, they should probably be closer to Ira Berlin's exhaustively annotated and interpreted *Freedom: A Documentary History of Emancipation, 1861-1867* than to John R. Commons' minimally annotated *Documentary History of American Industrial Society (1918-1935)*. Clear and extensive commentary and interpretive material will be needed because of the variety of the documents themselves and the need to analyze what they mean. Moreover, such commentary and interpretation will serve a broad audience. Everyone from advanced scholars writing monographs to high school students preparing term papers should be able to use these volumes.

A documentary history of the immigration experience is a project that has been on the fire, albeit often on a back burner, since 1986. Now that the Statue of Liberty has been renovated and Ellis Island has been restored and interpreted for visitors, the time is right for the members of the Statue of Liberty/Ellis Island History Committee and all others wishing to be involved to turn their attention from bricks and mortar to books and documents. We need to decide what the best format would be and how to organize our efforts to produce the volumes and cassettes and photographs and microforms that will allow the foreign-born makers of America's past to speak across time and space in their own words to this and future generations.

Notes

1. Robert Coles, "Introduction," in June Namias, *First Generation: In the Words of Twentieth Century American Immigrants* (Boston, 1978), xi.

2.   Rudolph J. Vecoli, "Ethnicity: A Neglected Dimension of American History," in *The State of American History*, ed. Herbert J. Bass (Chicago, 1970), 70-88.

3.   Rudolph J. Vecoli, presidential address delivered at the annual meeting of the Immigration History Society, Minneapolis, 20 April 1985, and published as "Return to the Melting Pot: Ethnicity in the United States in the Eighties," *Journal of American Ethnic History*, 5 (Fall 1985), 7-20. Vecoli remains in light of the rich historical scholarship in the 1980s, see Vecoli, "From *The Uprooted* to *The Transplanted*: The Writing of American Immigration History, 1951-1989," in Valeria Gennaro Lerda, ed. *From 'Melting Pot' to Multiculturalism: The Evolution of Ethnic Relations in the United States and Canada*, Estratto, Biblioteca Cultura 418 (1990), 25-53.

4.   An especially useful anthology of this kind is Moses Rischin, *Immigration and the American Tradition* (Indianapolis, 1976). Others are Stanley Feldstein and Lawrence Costello, eds. *The Ordeal of Assimilation: A Documentary History of the White Working Class, 1930s to the 1970s* (Garden City, N.Y., 1974) and Salvatore LaGumina and Frank J. Cavaioli, eds. *The Ethnic Dimension in American Society* (Boston, 1974) and a revised edition renamed *The Peripheral Americans* (Malabar, Florida, 1984).

5.   There are many collections of documents and letters available that offer the perspective of individual immigrants on their group's experience. Perhaps the best of these remains, Charlotte Erickson, *Invisible Immigrants; The Adaptation of English and Scottish Immigrants in Nineteenth-Century America* (Leicester, 1972). Others include: on the Eastern European Jews, Irving Howe and Kenneth Libo, *How We Lived: A Documentary History of Immigrant Jews in America, 1880-1930* (New York, 1979), Isaac Metzker, *A Bintel Brief, Sixty Years of Letters from the Lower East Side to the "Jewish Daily Forward"* (New York, 1972) and *A Bintel Brief, Volume II, Letters to the "Jewish Daily Forward," 1950-1980* (New York, 1981); on the Norwegians, Solveig Zempel, *"In Their Own Words'" Letters from Norwegian Immigrants* (Minneapolis, 1991); on the Chinese, Him Mark Lai, Genny Lim, Judy Yung, *Island, Poetry and History of Chinese Immigrants on Angel Island, 1910-1940* (San Francisco, 1980) and Marlon K. Hom, *Songs of the Golden Mountain, Cantonese Rhymes from San Francisco Chinatown* (Berkeley, 1987).

6.   Him Mark Lai et al., *Island*, 102.

7.   Thus far two volumes have appeared, with Series II preceding Series I into print. Ira Berlin, ed. *Freedom: A Documentary History of Emancipation, 1861-1867*, Series II *The Black Military Experience* (Cambridge, England, 1982) and Series I *The Destruction of Slavery* (Cambridge, England, 1985).

8.   Harmut Keil and John B. Jentz, eds. *German Workers in Chicago: A Documentary History of Working-Class Culture from 1850 to World War I* (Urbana, Illinois, 1988), 10-11.

Voice for the Voiceless: A Means to an End

Mary Lynn McCree Bryan

The task before me—that of making recommendations about the administrative structures and funding required to achieve *A Documentary History of American Immigration*—should be approached only after the work itself has been designed and the project's expected results have been identified. At this point, November 1990, I know only that there is to be a work. I am uncertain about its contents, its comprehensiveness, design, or audience. Let me proceed by making some assumptions.

In defining the work, I shall try to be conservative and assume a more complex ultimate goal than may actually result. The work will be composed of separate documentary histories presented by nationality group. Each may be a multimedia publication in which printed volumes and microform will dominate. The word "documents" will be broadly defined to include not only untranslated and translated texts, but also audiovisual evidence of the literature and art, including photographs, crafts, and drama, of each national group. All publications will be selective rather than comprehensive. The volume or volumes will be illustrated and scholarly in their editorial presentation. They will appeal to students and other scholars, as well as to a general reading public.

To preserve options for comparative study and to maintain a consistent scholarly design for the whole work, documents for each ethnic history will be presented in pre-determined, parallel categories and with similar editorial apparatus. Yet there will be space in each work for the editor to include special categories of documentation revealing of experiences or conditions unique to each national group. Music, interviews, speeches, or plays, on CD or tape with appropriate explanatory comments may be used to illustrate documentary texts, adding a reality and richness that printed material sometimes lacks. A more comprehensive documentary facsimile edition, on microform, and perhaps eventually on optic disc, with suitable finding aids would permit each editor to publish valuable data for scholars that could not be included in the more selective printed volumes.

And so for each nationality group I have supposed a combination of final product that could consist of one or more volumes, a facsimile publication, and an audiovisual package. Now, can we manage and afford it all?

Let's try to plan backwards and see. Let me identify and discuss some elements present in most large documentary projects that act as constraints affecting progress and success. The elements are: 1) the capabilities, experience, and coordination of the editorial team, including the editor, staff, consultants, and advisers; 2) the environment in which the project is conducted, including institutional home and the support of other scholars; 3) legal access to, as well as the quantity and quality of, the materials from which the works will be created; 4) the commitment of the publishers and the mechanism for marketing project publications; 5) the amount of time required to complete each project as well as available financial or in-kind support; and 6) an appropriate and cohesive general program design.

No matter what the number of volumes, one or more, these editions are unlikely to be the timely result of a solo editor's efforts. Experience among documentary editors indicates that with a complex publication goal and a large amount of documentation to consider, a team approach may be preferable. The editor who must gather and direct his or her team of scholar editors should be expert in the language, culture, and history of the ethnic group to be presented and should have the creative ability and vision to take documentation and direct its preparation for successful presentation to the audiences for which it is intended. He or she must be willing to commit a number of years to the project. Helping to devise an editorial apparatus; collecting, organizing, selecting, and preparing for publication the most significant and revealing documentation; fund raising; promoting the project; directing the work of the editorial team; and working with editorial board and publishers are all part of the editor's responsibilities. How well these tasks are integrated, how well they are done in a timely manner affect the success of the project. We need a mechanism for selecting the best editor for each segment of the work.

The composition of the editorial team will vary depending upon the design of the final product; the amount, type, and complexity of the material the project will consider; and the editor's style of work and expertise. In most cases, the team should consist of at least one administrative employee, and no less than one other full-time scholar editor. In various phases of each project, different skills may be required and so team members may change. The team may increase and decrease in size, too. Editors may choose to use consultants or special editors to complete audiovisual presentations and to assist with translation. In some cases, a project might want to include a special microform editor and staff.

Each editor should select a small editorial board of no more than eight or nine, consisting of appropriate scholars and persons with access to funding sources. It should assist in evaluating the proposed publications and developing financial support for the project. Scholars on the board should share the editor's vision of the work, and act constructively as critical evaluators. Those appointed for their access to potential support should be committed to the editor's vision of the work and be willing to open doors and speak effectively on its behalf. During the life of the project, the editorial board might meet once or more, or never, but the editor should be able to call upon individuals or a committee of its members as needed.

Asking one institution to host the entire immigrant experience project would be a huge commitment, and so I envision individual nationality segments lodged at separate institutions. It is best to keep the same hopefully supportive home institution for the life of each project segment. An ideal site for an editorial project would be in an institution that is building an archive relating to that national group. The editorial staff would have at hand a pool of material some of which would almost certainly be described and organized, making the selection process easier. In addition, being associated with an established, reliable collecting and preservation program might make it easier for the editorial team to identify and gather new materials. The repository would also likely already have, or be committed to building, a solid library of secondary and reference works relating to the nationality group, a must for the editorial project.

Besides adequate space, equipment, storage facilities, and access to telephone and copying, the home institution should also be expected to provide financial accounting for the project and access for the editorial team to a suitable fringe benefit package. In many cases, home institutions signify to potential funding agencies their commitment to a project by providing some or all of the salary of one of its employees.

Editorial projects with that kind of assistance are fortunate. Not all have it, and that is one of the weaknesses of those projects. The editor often spends a considerable amount of time trying to secure sufficient operating funds for the project, including his or her own salary. If not successful, the project could disintegrate before it has published. Then scholars might have no access to the data on which the editors have been working, and funding agencies would have wasted their previous support. To give the immigration experience projects the best chance of avoiding this situation, I strongly recommend that home institutions be asked to supply more than 50% of the editor's salary. That way, even if a project loses all save its institutional support, it can limp forward at the hands of the one person who should have the vision and the expertise to carry on.

Also vital is support for the project and its publications among scholars in appropriate and allied disciplines. Through announcements, papers,

101

reports, and articles, most will have enough knowledge of the project to be positive about it and its usefulness when asked their opinion by publishers and potential funders.

The document selection process is at the heart of any small, highly selective edition. All editors will want to have as large a quality collection of documents as possible from which to make their selections for publications. This, more than anything else, argues for coordination of archival and editing projects for the same national group. At the minimum, editors will want to choose materials for which copyright is or can be cleared and that fit the designated categories. Preference should be given to documentation of unquestioned authenticity that has not previously been published and that is highly representative or unique. Each editor owes the project a respectful and fresh look at all of the materials reasonably available.

Documentation should be accurately, and eloquently, presented, with sufficient editorial apparatus and explanation to make each piece useful. The minimalist view of annotation in vogue just now among many editors and funding programs should be applied by these project editors carefully and thoughtfully. All must keep in balance the necessity of letting the items speak for themselves and supporting them with adequate information, so that they are understood rather than misunderstood by those who will likely use them. The quality and relevance of the material, as well as its presentation, are major determinates of a positive response to the works by the academic community and public.

No matter how much effort is spent in preparing the works, if they find no ready market through library use or sales they will not be as successful as they should be. A publication and marketing plan is essential for this documentary history project. One publisher should present all of the printed volumes as part of the same series. Other appropriate publishers should issue microform, tape or CD publications. All publishing contracts should be negotiated by one authority representing the whole project. All royalties should be designated for use by the project and devoted to production of future segments. We should hope that all publications can be produced without need for subvention, yet we should also expect that the price of each will be kept as reasonable as possible.

Of course, there are traditional scholarly markets: libraries, historical agencies, and individual scholars; but what about reaching the general public? Paperback editions, cassettes, and CDs appeal to all. These could be sold through bookshops; appropriate specialty, souvenir, and gift stores; historical societies; or sites like Ellis Island, The Statue of Liberty, and the Smithsonian. Members of cultural organizations associated with each nationality group seem likely purchasers for the publications, too. Each editorial team must stand ready to play its role in the marketing process. We must not ignore the potentially large foreign market, either. The series publishers should have the capacity and network to gain access to all segments of that market.

Now, to financial support. Unless each segment of the total project is designed so that it can be successfully completed in a reasonable time by a solo editor, requiring little or no support, someone will have to develop resources sufficient to see each part of the project to its conclusion. Ideally, someone will step forward at the start, giving assurance of adequate support for a number of years and guaranteeing continuity to completion. A shining example of such an arrangement is the Woodrow Wilson Papers, whose editor and staff have worked steadily, churning out volumes without the threat that pending lack of support poses. Their funds are provided entirely by the Woodrow Wilson Foundation and Princeton University. Unfortunately, that kind of commitment seems highly unlikely to materialize for this project. Most projects must seek support as they go. All staff, consultants, and advisers are paid from grant money as are all expenses, including equipment purchase, services, travel, supplies, and copying. As I pointed out earlier, many must secure even the editor's salary each year from sources outside their institutional homes. And the editor is the chief fund raiser.

There is great appeal in keeping salaries and expenses on projects at the minimum. Depending on budget size, institutional support, and the response of potential outside sources of support, more than 50% of an editor's time can be spent in fund raising activities. That usually means less time spent in editing and a longer time to project completion. We need a project structure that permits editors to edit more and fund raise less.

How much money does this whole project or even one segment of it need? Salary, fringe and expenses for a four-FTE-person staff (editor, associate or assistant editor, administrative assistant, and part-time assistants or consultants) could consume at least $150,000 a year in direct costs. But there is also the matter of indirect costs. Indirect costs are usually at least 50-60% of direct costs. Unless the home institution is willing to waive all or a large portion, the indirect cost component of any project budget increases by more than one half the amount of money a project staff must raise. At 60%, the indirect costs on a $150,000 budget are $90,000, bringing the total annual budget to $240,000.

And that's only the first year. What of the second, third, fourth years—or longer? Project salaries and costs keep escalating, too. Each project could easily require $1,000,000 before the end of five years, and the editorial staff may not have issued all of its publications. Let's try to be pragmatic. How much time can we reasonably give each project? Where can we get the support we need?

Of course, we will expect home institution support to reduce the amount of direct and indirect costs associated with each project. What is left over will have to be funded from other sources, which are primarily public and private foundations, individuals, and a variety of businesses and civic and cultural organizations in the United States and abroad. It is important to remember that any funding strategy must include a means for coordinating the funding efforts of the editing and archival components of concurrent operating segments of the national program.

The most obvious sources for additional support are the NHPRC and the NEH. Neither agency is a sure bet. Both are subject to the vicissitudes of the national budget process and re-authorization legislation. Either agency could simply cease to exist, or could have more or less money than before, or have no money at all. Proposals submitted to them are subjected to staff and board review as well as to a peer review process. Neither agency may be willing or able to provide all of the funding needed after institutional support has been established. In the recent past, many successful NEH proposals in the editions program have been awarded a combination of matching and outright funds. In my experience, the outright portion has always been the lesser of the two. Some projects may receive support from both NEH and NHPRC. Unfortunately, other government funds do not count toward meeting the NEH matching requirement.

To secure the NEH match, a project must develop new funding from private sources. One immediately thinks of private and business foundations. The large ones that fund projects in the humanities are obvious to all of us. Ford, MacArthur, Rockefeller, Pew, and Mellon, to name a few. The thousands of smaller foundations specializing in specific giving areas are difficult and time consuming to identify and approach successfully. Many of them make awards of $10,000 or less. And since the time it takes to request $100,000 is often the same as that it takes to ask for $10,000, it only makes sense to explore the $100,000 sources first.

Yet, there will certainly be some foundations that support activities relating to specific nationality groups. Once identified, these offer great opportunities for the immigrant history projects. For example, the Charles H. Revson Foundation makes awards for Jewish history, and the Siragusa & Delmas foundations for Italian, the Tinker for Spanish, and the Glencoe Foundation for Scottish-related projects.

One of the problems with private foundations is that most seem to make one-time awards. Therefore it will be important to request sufficient funding the first time for the anticipated length of the project or to devise some strategy of approach that will make the most of this practice.

One strategy successfully tried by other documentary editors is the use of a consortium. In most, though not all cases, this strategy has resulted in large multi-year awards shared by the projects that have joined together in the consortium to cooperate rather than compete in seeking financial assistance. The cooperative nature of the approach provides more access to funding agencies than individual projects are likely to develop on their own and permits a project access to a foundation it has been forbidden to approach by its home institution. It seems appealing to foundations, too. Three consortia that have had more than a little success are the Founding Fathers, Inc., the women's projects and the blacks' projects.

By far the most successful has been the Founding Fathers, Inc., receiving $1,500,000 each from the Mellon and Pew foundations. The $3,000,000 was to be used in conjunction with other funding over a multi-year period to benefit the Washington, Franklin, Jefferson, Adams, and Madison projects. The same consortium was not as successful on its second approach, receiving $250,000 from one foundation and a grant of $1,500,000 from the other.

Other options for support are individuals, businesses, and civic and cultural organizations with a natural affinity for the project. The Statue of Liberty/Ellis Island Foundation has already identified many of them. It should be willing to lend its considerable support and experience on behalf of this project. Developing gifts from individuals is usually very time consuming and unpredictable in its success. Some few projects have received unsolicited gifts from individuals, but more have worked extremely hard at cultivating prospects to collect only a few hundred dollars for their time. Taking every reasonable opportunity to generate positive publicity on all media, through publications, articles, appearances, speeches, and exhibits can only help the project's cause. The more relevant the project seems to the largest possible number of people the more likely it is to receive support.

And what of potential sources outside of America? That is less clear to me, but certainly worth exploring. There must be private sources of capital in many of the countries from which our immigrant wealth came. We need to identify likely sources and develop access to them. The real question is the degree to which such an appeal would be successful. The same time might be more productively spent in this country. However, there are avenues I would definitely explore. Among them, approaching cultural attachés in appropriate embassies and the foundations of multi-national businesses active in the United States, no matter where they are headquartered, in this country or abroad. Coming quickly to mind are Japanese auto and electronics firms, German automakers, and Italian furniture manufacturers.

The whole immigration experience project can only be costly. If we consider that it could take at least ten years to complete each ethnic group history the way I have defined the publications, and that each will cost no less than $2,000,000, then we can get a measure of the support this project must receive to succeed: $20,000,000 to complete the histories of ten ethnic groups, $40,000,000 for twenty. And that includes no adjustment for inflation, which could be a significant factor since the projects will have to be carried out over a period of twenty years or more. To secure funding of this sort for documentary history is an awesome task. Is the U.S. Congress a possibility?

Do we need to think smaller? If the editor does not participate in a search for materials, but rather waits to select materials from among those identified or gathered by the archival projects, perhaps the time and funding necessary for each editorial project could be cut by several years. It is difficult to judge with any accuracy the amount of time a complex project will require. Time to completion is, in large part, a function of unknown outside events as well as funding available, the skills, work time, number and duties of the editorial team, the search, the condition and amount of the materials, and the publication design.

If only one volume for each nationality group were approved and no other publication, perhaps each editorial team could complete their task in three years. That would considerably reduce the funding required. Would such a publication be adequate and acceptable? That may be thinking too small.

To tie all these elements I've been talking about together successfully, we must create an effective organizational structure headed by an advisory board that will:

1) approve the project design;
2) provide a means for selecting the best project personnel;
3) coordinate and secure adequate funding as well as in-kind resources including home institutional support;
4) permit editorial personnel to edit in preference to fund raising;
5) negotiate the best possible publishing contract or contracts;
6) promote the project and its publications;

7) encourage ease of access for all national segments of the project to sufficient quality materials from which to create publications;
8) manage cooperation among nationality segments and between archival and editorial components of the projects; and
9) monitor and evaluate project progress.

The project should be carried out either under the aegis of an already established organization, like the Ellis Island/Statue of Liberty Foundation, or a university or research institution like the Newberry Library of Chicago, or it may be possible to create a new independent legal entity. Of these three options, I prefer the first or second. The organization chosen would be responsible for hosting and supporting the advisory board and its staff, if there is any. The project advisory board should be composed of individuals with access to potential funding sources and the media as well as of an assortment of appropriate and experienced archivists, documentary editors, and historians. The board should have no more than seventeen members. It should have diversity yet not be too cumbersome or too expensive to operate.

Two small working committees of the board should specialize on 1) project design and publication and 2) fund raising. For example, unless this meeting or its planning committee identifies the specific ethnic segments of the whole project to be undertaken and defines the contents for each publication, a committee of the project advisory board may have to decide those issues.

Advisory board members, serving without pay, could be chosen in a variety of ways. Representatives appointed by nationality group organizations or by professional academic organizations would probably not create the kind of cohesive, committed group this board should be. Academic board members should be chosen in large part from among those planning the work. Promotion and fund raising members might be selected from among influential individuals who have supported other similar ventures or who profess a commitment to the project. The host institution should actually make the advisory board appointments. Five-year terms, renewable once, should be staggered. Continuity is important to this project.

The advisory board head or president or perhaps general editor should maintain communication among project segments and with board members, and coordinate appropriate fund raising efforts. Editorial control of each nationality segment will rest with the editor of that segment, with his or her team and editorial board, who will work with the project advisory board through its head and its committees. Depending upon the final project design and the responsibilities of the advisory board, its leader may be so busy that he or she will have to commit to a part-time appointment and receive salary. The advisory board will probably also require the assistance of a part-time administrative secretary. Costs must be kept as low as possible. Fund raising should support the individual projects rather than the advisory board function. The full advisory board may meet only once a year, but there must be some funds available for working committee meetings, especially at the start.

These bare bones of a coordinating organization may be totally inadequate. But, I present them as a jumping-off-place for discussion purposes. No matter whether the projects are to result in multimedia publications or one or two volumes, the immigrant experience project will require a coordinating organization. It must be equal to the task and smooth and consistent in operation. Whatever the structure that results from our deliberations, operating the project must consume far less than ten percent of available funding; it must not be the tail that wags the dog. It is the excellence of each nationality segment on which success should rest. It's time to see what we can do to help the voiceless speak.